OTHELLO:

AN HISTORICAL AND COMPARATIVE STUDY

BY

ELMER EDGAR STOLL, Ph.D.
Professor of English in the University of Minnesota.

GORDIAN PRESS, INC.
NEW YORK
1967

PR
2829
.S75
1967

Originally Published 1915
Reprinted 1967

Published by Gordian Press, Inc,

Library of Congress Catalog Card Number 67-21714

Printed in U.S.A. by
EDWARDS BROTHERS, INC.
Ann Arbor, Michigan

CONTENTS

TABLE OF EDITIONS TO WHICH REFERENCE IS MADE

The text of the Globe edition of Spenser (Macmillan & Co., 1902) has been used in this dissertation.

The following books have been used in the editions here specified: —

Brut Tysilio, translated by Peter Roberts, 1811, under the title, *The Chronicle of the Kings of Britain.*

Camden, William, *Britannia,* 1590.

Fabyan, Robert, *The New Chronicles of England and France,* ed. Sir Henry Ellis, London, 1811.

Geoffrey of Monmouth, *Historia Regum Britanniae,* ed. San Marte, Halle, 1854.

Grafton, Richard, *Chronicle at Large* . . . ed. Sir Henry Ellis, London, 1809.

Hardyng, John, *Chronicle,* ed. Sir Henry Ellis, London, 1812.

Higden, Ralph, *Polychronicon,* ed. in the Rolls Series, vols. I and II by C. Babington, vols. III–IX by J. R. Lumby, 1865–1886.

Holinshed, Raphael, *Chronicles,* 1577.[1]

Laʒamon, *Brut,* ed. Sir Fred. Madden, 3 vols., London, 1847.

Mannyng, Robert, of Brunne, *Chronicle,* ed. Furnivall, Rolls Series, 2 vols., 1887.

"Matthew of Westminster," *Flores Historiarum,* ed. H. R. Luard, Rolls Series, London, 1890.

Mirror for Magistrates, ed. Joseph Haslewood, 3 vols., London, 1815.

Paris, Matthew, *Chronica Majora,* ed. H. R. Luard, Rolls Series, London, 1872.

Polydore Vergil, *Anglicae Historiae Libri XXVI,* English

---

[1] When the edition of 1587 has been used it is specified in the footnote.

translation, ed. from MS. of the time of Henry VII, by Sir Henry Ellis, Camden Society, London, 1846.

Rastell, John, *The Pastime of People,* ed. Dibden, London, 1811.

" Robert of Gloucester," *Chronicle,* ed. W. A. Wright, Rolls Series, 2 vols., 1887.

Stow, John, *Annales* . . . Augmented by Edmund Howes, London, 1631.

Warner, William, *Albions England,* London, 1612.

OTHELLO

I hope that the reader will bear with me while so familiar a figure as Othello is, at such length, discussed once again. Hitherto he has hardly been studied in the light of Comparative Literature; hitherto he has hardly been studied even as a bit of Elizabethan art. But the problems of one play are, in varying degrees, those of other plays like it, whether Shakespearean or merely Elizabethan, whether modern or ancient; and art, not life, furnishes the clearer and more pertinent comment on art, problems the only solution to problems. Chief among these in the play before us are certain relations of character to plot, and the measure of the dramatist's concern for the consistency of his characters, and of his interest, conscious or instinctive, in what is nowadays called psychology. And these we shall prove to have been studying only in all their extension and amplitude, I hope, at moments when we may have seemed to be wandering afield. A precise and formal unity does not greatly concern us: in order to get at the truth about Othello we shall examine many another character, and we hope to get at the truth about many another character in examining Othello. Really, not the Moor, but the art with which he is exhibited, is our theme.

"One defect in the play which has been felt by all critics," says Lewes, in 1875, in the essay on *Actors and the Art of Acting,* "is the rapidity with which Othello is made to believe in his wife's guilt." A very few of the critics have even said that they felt it. Among these are dramatic critics so enlightened as Bulthaupt and Mr. William Archer—"Othello, when we look into it," says the latter, "succumbs with incredible facility,"[1]—as well as literary critics such as Snider and Mr. Frank Harris. If nothing else, they have for their warrant the repeated utterances in the text itself—Emilia's, Desdemona's, Iago's, Othello's own. According to these, and in keeping with the actual presentation of the character, the hero is "not easily jealous," not jealous by nature, and yet, within a single scene, he becomes jealous terribly, irrecoverably, as no man ever was. Indeed, as at least two of the

---

[1] *Playmaking* (1912), p. 202.

critics seem to have recognized, the character is inconsistent not at this point only but throughout.

> The Moor is of a free and open nature,
> That thinks men honest that but seem to be so;

yet in trusting his cynical subaltern, who has not been on terms of friendship with him, he thereby distrusts his dearest friend and his newly wedded wife. He is one, says Lodovico, "whom passion could not shake"—"Can he be angry?" asks even Iago in wonder,[1]—and up to the moment of Cassio's disgrace, in fact, one might say up to the moment of temptation, never was there, in trying circumstances, anyone so serene, disengaged, and dignified as he; yet, at a man's word, he falls a prey to the wildest and grossest of passions, cries aloud for "blood," vows to "tear her all to pieces," "chop her into messes," and throw her lover's "nose to the dogs," and forthwith seeks the death of both. He is a general of renown, "the noble Moor whom our full Senate call all in all sufficient," and in Venice, even in the opinion of his unadmiring Ancient, "another of his fathom they have none to lead their business," his mind being no less ample than his heart; yet so tamely, so precipitately—without judgment, consideration of evidence, or perception of character, whether Iago's, Cassio's, or his wife's—does he succumb to covert suggestion and open slander and every stratagem brought to bear, that critics of such eminence as Mr. Stopford Brooke have been driven to cry, with Emilia, "O gull, O dolt, as ignorant as dirt," and ascribe his fall chiefly to his lack of wit. He is, as men go, pure in heart, all for war and not a bit for amorous self-indulgence, and "but that he loved the gentle Desdemona he would not have put his unhousèd, free condition into conscription and confine for the sea's worth," begs that she may accompany him to Cyprus, not to please the palate of his appetite, but to be free and bounteous to her mind, and hastens away to war, "this night" and "with all his heart," without her; yet he is presently filled with sensual imaginings, and treats Desdemona as "a cunning whore of Venice," and Emilia as her go-between, in so far that the moralizing Snider[2] and Heraud[3] are persuaded that the root of the trouble is that he has all the suspiciousness of a guilty conscience

---

[1] III, 4, 134ff. Iago knows better, of course, from recent experience, but he seems in these lines to be playing innocent on the strength of Othello's known reputation, if indeed his speech be not merely a *mot d'auteur*.

[2] Snider (*System,* i. p. 111) and Gervinus (Eng. ed. 1877, pp. 510, 530), touch upon the contradiction but devise no means to obviate it.

[3] Furness, Variorum *Othello,* p. 422, where Heraud infers from the scene in which Othello throws his purse to Emilia that he had indeed "poured his treasures into foreign laps," had been no celibate, and by this inlet had suffered suspicion and jealousy to enter in. One wonders how many of Shakespeare's unmarried heroes would have turned out to be celibate had the poet been interested enough to say. The question troubled Dumas *fils* in so far as it concerned the heroes of Molière. For big or little, Dumas or Heraud, it has great importance today. But for Molière or Shakespeare the question would probably have been, not whether the character was chaste or celibate, but whether he was an ascetic or a libertine.

and that the Ancient's doubts concerning him and Emilia are reasonable and just.

What is to be made, we ask ourselves, of this great heap of contradictions? Critics have been stumbling at them, more or less unconsciously, ever since the days of Rymer, but Bulthaupt and Mr. Frank Harris seem to be the only ones who have quite opened their eyes and seen. "The truth of the matter is that in the beginning of the play Othello is a marionette fairly well shaped and exceedingly picturesque; but as soon as jealousy is touched upon the mask is thrown aside: Othello the self-contained captain disappears, the poet takes his place," etc. And on the truth of the matter Mr. Harris may there have laid his finger, although he proceeds to take this inconsistency, like every other in a Shakespearean hero, for an intrusion of the poet's personality, and for the moment seems strangely blind to the beauty of the chief figure in the play.

Bulthaupt contents himself with demonstrating that Othello's precipitate credulity is unmotived.[1] Everybody else, so far as I am aware, has recourse to some one or other of the approved means for preserving to us a Shakespearean character's dubious identity—Fate or a distracted order of society, the all-compelling arts of the villain, the blinding of passion, the extraordinary circumstances of the marriage, racial and social characteristics and differences, Desdemona's duplicity, the hero's or heroine's stupidity, or (taking the bull fairly by the horns) mere psychology itself. Another interpretation, which explains, but makes no attempt to explain away, the contradiction, is, that we have here the simple convention of the calumniator believed, as old as the story of Potiphar's wife or of the wicked counselors of Germanic heroic legend, which, though modified, constantly reappears in drama, ancient, Elizabethan, or modern, down almost to Ibsen's day.[2]

Accustomed to modern methods of dramatic art, which involve analysis and psychology, the critics, naturally enough, cannot conceive of a man so readily becoming suspicious and violently passionate and sensual, stupid or bereft of dignity, without being such at bottom from the first. Especially has this been the case with the Germans. With Schlegel, they have taken the Moor's dignity and virtue for the crust of discipline and Venetian culture, through which might break, at any moment, the red lava of sexual passion and barbarism, or, with Gervinus, Ulrici, and Wetz, have thought that his later passions were within him, though in the germ. One of them has

---

[1] *Dramaturgie des Schauspiels* (1894), ii, p. 224.

[2] *Modern Philology*, July, 1912, my article, "Criminals in Shakespeare and Science," p. 75.— Saben, counselor to Hugdietrich, and Sibich, counselor to Ermanrich, are like the Sir Aldingar of the old ballad, and like many another in balladry and legend mentioned by Child in his introduction, ii. pp. 33-34. So far as mere evidence goes, Aldingar is almost as well provided as Iago. He puts the leper in the Queen's bed and brings the King to see, while Iago gets the handkerchief into Cassio's hand. And the King, like Othello, will not give ear either to his wife or to him who is supposed to be her companion in crime.

even found *den stürmischen Ausbruch seines Innern* in the Moor's speeches
to the Signoria,[1] the calmest and serenest, perhaps, that the poet ever penned
Others, and many Englishmen with them, have tried to bridge the chasm by
insisting on the extraordinary and ticklish nature of the union, fitted to
keep the black man uneasy and anxious, or have taken refuge in that which
explains and rationalizes anything—the finger of Fate, or the cloud of
passion, which seals up Othello's eyes alike to Desdemona's virtue and Iago's
villainy, to say nothing of the weak spots in Iago's plot. What in Anglo-
Saxon countries at least may be called the orthodox theory, however, is that
in the first act and up to the temptation scene Shakespeare had fashioned a
free and perfect soul, with no weakness but his trustfulness (if a weakness
that be), and that he fell only by that and by Iago's guile. Such is the
theory of Coleridge,—"a conviction forced upon him by the superhuman
art of Iago, such a conviction as any man would and must have entertained
who had believed Iago's honesty as Othello did;"[2]—and in the main it is
held by Hazlitt, Ulrici and Gervinus, Dr. Brandes, Professors Bradley,
Raleigh, Schelling, Thorndike, Wolff, and others. They are truer to the
text than the rest, but as psychological, and far less logical and plausible in
their psychology. They lightly take it that by insisting on the supremacy and
malignity of Iago's art, the Moor's unsuspiciousness and the tenderness and
"vulnerability of the point of attack"—his trustfulness and his love for his
wife—"every step of the appalling chain of intrigue becomes the natural out-
come of the motives of the persons before you."[3] So far as Othello is concerned this might be the case if it were merely a struggle in which goodness
is attacked by evil—if the Moor were not a great self-respecting personality
instead of a subject for hypnosis—if the virtue (or weakness) of trustfulness, as well as his love, did not require *a fortiori* that he should trust his
wife and friend at least as well as a stranger—if all his virtues, his intelligence, and the dignity of his character and position did not require that he
should brush aside Iago's legerdemain of innuendo and mystery-mongering
at a stroke, instead of being held fascinated from the beginning as is a bird
or a monkey by a serpent. Their psychology simply pushes back the paradox a degree, instead of abolishing it; their psychology presumes that innocence inclines to a belief in guilt, rather than to a belief in innocence,
and that the most trustful man is most capable of distrust.[4] If there is any
psychology in the play, this, to be sure, it must be; but I cannot see that
there is any more than in the dictum of Iago, which takes it all for granted—

> The Moor is of a free and open nature
> That thinks men honest that but seem to be so—

[1] E. Traumann, *Jahrbuch*, xxxi, p. 257.
[2] *Lectures on Shakespeare* (Bohn ed.), p. 393.
[3] A. H. Thorndyke, *Tragedy*, pp. 162-4.
[4] See below, *passim*.

and summarily, theatrically lifts and floats us over contradiction and paradox as over a rock in the river. Here is a working formula, a postulate or fundamental premise, which then did not demand or provoke investigation; and more than that the dramatist did not contemplate or require.[1]

It is profitable to turn from the theories of critics, however, to the practice of playwrights. In *Much Ado* as in *Cymbeline*, in Greene's *Orlando Furioso* as in Beaumont and Fletcher's *Philaster* or even Dryden's *Conquest of Granada,* the blameless hero, like Othello, blamably, unpsychologically believes whatever the slanderer (and the poet) would have him believe. All his intelligence and his nobility of soul, all his knowledge of his beloved's character and ignorance of the slanderer's, avail him nothing. Angelica's father and her lover Orlando cast her off on hearsay, without a word of questioning, or any remembrance of the purity of her past, not to believe in her again until the slander is contradicted by the witch Melissa, in Act Five. Claudio, trusting mere appearances and the testimony of a man who, he rightly thinks, "loves him not," "shames" Hero in the church (even the lady's father siding with him) without warning or word in private. Posthumus, accepting the circumstantial report of the stranger Iachimo without troubling to return, sends out of Italy orders for his lady's death. Philaster, though for the looks of things he draws his sword when Dion slanders Arethusa, fully credits the slander afterwards, and when he speaks to her and the boy, shows no trace of the spirit of inquiry but is deaf to all that they can say. And in Dryden's heroic drama the husband and the lover are still quicker to think the worst, and the husband would have his wife to the stake out of hand.[2] So, in a single scene, without giving his wife or his friend a hearing, Othello is led to the point of wishing to "tear her all to pieces," shouting "blood, blood, blood," and vowing, in company with Iago, the death of both; and though later he questions Desdemona and her woman, he is, like Philaster and Dolce's Herod, blind, deaf, and obdurate. And the passion of the heroes (Claudio of course is without it and Orlando's turns his wits) is, while it runs its course, made as violent and brutal as it is abrupt and unreasonable, and abounds in sensual imaginings and in outcries

---

[1] It cannot be too much insisted upon that the paradox was not intended. It appears in Othello, as in Falstaff, only when he is considered psychologically, having fallen into a critic's hands. See Morgann's *Essay on the Dramatic Character of Sir John Falstaff,* and my article, "Falstaff," *Modern Philology,* October, 1914, p. 66 *et seq.* "A fierce thing made weak by his very strength," says Dowden; but such a problem is altogether out of the circle of Shakespeare's theatrical, unphilosophical art. He shows no consciousness of it, makes nothing of it, and paradoxes in character are not to be found, for that matter, even in Ibsen. The true parallel to the paradox in Othello lies in the other noble heroes made jealous, presently to be taken up, and in Masefield's Nan, below, pp. 51-2. Noble sentiments the dramatist seizes with one hand, murder with the other, and an indisputable dramatic effect with both. And to bring this to consummation, Shakespeare, in Othello and Posthumus, makes, by means of the omnipotent villain, his hero, who is not suspicious or jealous by nature, suspicious and jealous in fact, paradox or psychology never troubling or appearing.

[2] Pt. II, IV, iii, and V, i, Almanzor's soliloquy. The illustrations from romantic drama might be accumulated without end.

against woman and wedded life. But out of this obscuration and eclipse the hero's old self, like Othello's, ultimately emerges. Well before the play is over he comes to his senses again; and he has been made noble that he may be lovable, and his jealousy is not spontaneous, not born and bred within. Through an arbitrary but immemorial convention, it is instilled into his soul by a villain's wiles.

With or without sexual jealousy, the convention of the calumniator credited is one of the oldest traditions of the drama. It reappears in Shakespeare's next play, *King Lear*, when Gloster, quite without reason, implicitly takes the word of the bastard (who repeats some of Iago's tricks) though it blackens his better known and equally beloved son. Here and elsewhere, without either proof demanded or a hearing given, the noble, intelligent father, lover, or king straightway contrives or compasses the death of the acccused. The Viceroy in the *Spanish Tragedy* cries "Away with him!" the moment the slandered Alexander opens his mouth.[1] Theseus, in the tragedies of Euripides, Seneca, and Racine, once he has heard the charge, curses his son, and, claiming the promise of Poseidon, prays incontinently for his death.[2] Dolce's Tetrarch brings the charge himself and has no ears for anything but slander. And in Bounin's *Soltane* (1561) the despot simply wastes no words upon the matter but kills his son and heir at sight. No one, in fine, knows anyone, and short of the last scene of the last act anyone can be made to believe or disbelieve anything. And when one takes the notion to slander himself, charging himself, like Prince Malcolm, with every sin in the calendar, even a man of the world like Macduff must needs believe him, and at once disbelieve him again when all of it is unsaid.[3] What is said is everything—the matter too and not the manner[4]—when a situation is at stake. What Iago and Richard, Goneril and Regan, Edgar and Cordelia, all their lives long, have done or been, counts, at the crucial moment, as against what they are now feigning or dissembling, for nothing at all.[5] "Why let me see," says to himself Congreve's Maskwell, at a time when this ancient convention began to require a bit of explaining; "I have the same force, the same words and accents, when I speak what I do think, and when

---

[1] I, iii. In the Elizabethan drama such situations are not uncommon.

[2] *Phèdre* IV, ii. In Euripides and Seneca Theseus does not even wait till he has set eyes upon him. In Racine he asks what Phèdre meant by her vague and riddling words, and when Hippolyte chivalrously refers him to the lady herself, he takes the evidence of the sword, as Othello takes that of the handkerchief, and Oenone's report, as Othello Iago's.

[3] See below, p. 26, for Othello's disbelieving Iago as promptly as he believed in him, once the machinery is reversed. And compare Dekker's *Honest Whore*, Pt. II, III, i, where Infelice charges herself with incontinence in order to get her husband to commit himself, and then turns the charge against him instead. For Malcolm see *Macbeth*, IV, iii.

[4] The reason which Malcolm gives is the same as Iachimo's excuse when he withdraws his slanderous charges against Posthumus—the desire to put her to the proof—and if the speakers were flesh and blood, would, in either case, be superfluous or in vain. See below, p. 23, for the manners of honesty and dishonesty being the same.—*Cymbeline*, I, vi, 156-68.

[5] See below, p. 7 and p. 47.

I speak what I do not think—the very same—and dear dissimulation is the only art not to be known from nature." Proof or probability is not required.

Of slander bringing about jealousy there is found a more modern form in such plays as Voltaire's *Zaïre* and Schiller's *Kabale und Liebe,* where the villain's function in bringing about the catastrophe is encroached upon or supplanted by the use of evidence worthier the name—by an external obstacle like the oath sealing the lips of the accused, or by conduct even more imprudent than Desdemona's own. But even here, as in any other form of the convention (whether with jealousy or without) there is not lacking the presumption that lovers, husbands and wives, fathers and sons, have no confidence in one another and next to no acquaintance. The men are as incapable of interpreting evidence or taking counsel[1]—*tragische Verblendung,* the learned have it—as the women are of understanding what the men are about; and when the storm breaks these dodge the issue, weep or cower, or cry out "betrayed," "undone,"[2] instead of resting on their integrity and appearing as innocent as they are. Like Othello and Desdemona and the other Elizabethans, and Dolce's Herod[3] and Marianna, neither man nor wife can be said to seek an explanation of the other—not Orosmane or Zaïre,[4] not Luise or Ferdinand. Othello, Herod,[5] and Ferdinand, at least, are resolved upon the death of the beloved even before they confront her, they confront her only to bring the charge, and the charge is so vague, sweeping, and furious that the poor thing has no chance to comprehend, still less to answer, it. Again and again the plot hangs as by a thread, for Othello and Orosmane, Zaïre and Desdemona, evade the one issue which common sense requires them to face—the name of the paramour. Desdemona indeed once faces it:

> Des. To whom, my lord? With whom? How am I false?
> Oth. Oh Desdemona! Away! away! away!

But it is Othello himself who turns away, there he conveniently drops the matter, and not till the death scene, when (as Othello thinks) "his mouth is stopped," is the putative paramour's name once again upon their lips. All

---

[1] Once his own suspicions are aroused, Dolce's Herod, for instance, though the Cup-bearer has contradicted his testimony and confessed, simply will not hear the reasonable advice the Councillor is giving him at his elbow, and though he talks with the Queen, only brings accusations, never seeks the truth. So Othello turns a deaf ear to Emilia when he questions her, and, as Thésée does with Hippolyte (IV, 2), gets into a rage when Desdemona defends herself. (V, ii, 56 ff).

[2] Desdemona, V, ii, 76; Arethusa, *Philaster,* III, 2: "betrayed." Cf.*Kabale und Liebe,* V, 2: *Luise.* "Ich bin verloren, mich zu ermorden ist der da!" Ferdinand naturally takes it for a confession of guilt.

[3] See, end of Act II, his resolve on the strength of his new suspicions.

[4] They do at the earlier stages of the jealousy (like Luise, Zaïre is bound by an oath) but not after the intercepting of the letter.

[5] I refer to his second jealousy, after the Cup-bearer's testimony has broken down. See below, p. 21, and above, note 1.

this is, by present-day standards, little short of claptrap. And though Voltaire, too, once has his hero shy away from the rival's name,

l'insolent qui t'adore,[1]

he contrives, like Schiller, to thrust many of the difficulties out of character into the plot[2]—by means of the oath, the ambiguous letter, the naturally mistaken identity of the rival—provides the hero, as we said, with much better evidence and a stronger provocation, painstakingly motivates[3] his decision not to confront Zaïre with the letter in person, and even has him for a time allay his earlier jealousy, in part

by request and such fair question
As soul to soul affordeth;[4]

in part, as no other of these jealous heroes does, by looking in her face and bearing witness for himself to her purity and love:

Et son âme, éprouvant cette ardeur qui me touche,
Vingt fois pour me le dire a volé sur sa bouche. IV, 3.

Othello's

If she be false, O, then heaven mocks itself!
I'll not believe't .   .

has the striking theatrical effect, to be sure, which in the other is wanting, as well as passion and poetry; only, then and there he *does* believe it, immediately complains of his cuckold's forehead, and plunges headlong again into Iago's toils. Before this same scene is over he is raging for her blood, while Orosmane's recovery of faith, being more than a stage thrill or sensation, lasts until he receives the intercepted letter; and even then he does not condemn Zaïre until he hears how she in turn receives it, near the end. All of Othello's evidence (the dream and the mere loss of the handkerchief are as nothing compared to Desdemona's inexplicable conduct and what the madman thinks he hears Cassio say) comes after he is convinced and resolved; but Orosmane's, like Ferdinand's, all before.[5] That of itself might almost dispose of the psychology found lurking in the lines.

Whether in the older or the newer form, the tradition is even yet not extinct, but (however little that may mean to Shakespeare critics) it is now hopelessly discredited. The "wrongful assumption of guilt" is, once for all,

---

[1] *Zaïre,* IV, vi.

[2] See, below, the situation, which of itself provokes jealousy, without merely unreasonable conduct on the part of the characters.

[3] IV, v, by the counsel of Corasmin and by Orosmane's own pride.

[4] See, for examples, *Zaïre,* III, vi; IV, ii; vi.

[5] Nérestan's and Zaïre's affectionate interest and solitary conversations, Zaïre's inexplicable offishness and avoidance of her husband, the favors she begs for Nérestan, her boon of solitude for herself, the letter, and her going to the rendezvous.

listed as one of the seven "cardinal sins of the craft," along with the "aside, the soliloquy, impersonation, eaves-dropping, confidences, and the losing ef papers,"[1] or (one might add) of handkerchiefs. At the least, the char-acter, who assumes and suspects must now have the disposition rooted within him. How thoroughly external and unpsychological a device it is in Shakes-peare appears most clearly, perhaps, in the case of Gloster in *King Lear* and Leonato in *Much Ado,* who have of course no motive such as has been urged, though without reason, in Othello's defense—lack of acquaintance[2] or a pre-disposition to jealousy—but have been fond and indulgent fathers. Leonato, harkening to Claudio, will not harken to Beatrice or the Friar or Hero herself, as if he cherished a grudge against her ; and Gloster, giving heed to Edmund, is ready at once to make his lawful heir an outlaw and bring him to the stake.[3]

In Voltaire and Schiller the unnaturalness of the contrivance is, though less evident, not less real, then, than in Shakespeare and Beaumont and Fletcher; but in their hands the character of the hero is not twisted into a paradox. Orosmane and Ferdinand are jealous in their own right; and though the circumstances which induce suspicion are far more to the pur-pose, both dramatists take pains actually to show traces of the trait[4] before the jealousy begins. And there is no nightmare or eclipse of passion, out of which, at the end, the hero emerges with something of his pristine splendor, no grandiose dramatic effect such as that involved in the *Hercules Furens*—in Elizabethan times constantly, in various forms, repeated, though without a god for a cause—which more than atoned (if then, indeed, there was anything for which to atone) for the violence done the character. Neither Voltaire nor Schiller could take interest in a passion which is little less than a madness, whether coming as a visitation from on high or en-grafted by a villain's guile.

The practice of playwrights as regards the convention having been ex-amined, we now take up the various elements of the contradiction in Othello's character in order, jealousy first. Many critics, including Horn, Ulrici, Dowden, Hudson, Bulthaupt, and Dr. Eckhardt,[5] have followed Coleridge in denying that his passion is jealousy; others, including Vischer, Wetz, Wilson, Mr. Stopford Brooke, and Mr. Frank Harris have contended that it is nothing else. Still others take the jealousy for granted, or like Profes-

---

[1] W. L. George, *Dramatic Actualities* (1914), p. 6. Any student of the modern drama will recognize the truth of this at once.

[2] See below, pp. 47-8.

[3] *Lear,* II, i, 58-65.

[4] *Zaïre,* I, v, ll. 309-10.
   Je ne suis point jaloux . . . si je l'étais jamais.
   Si mon cœur . . . Ah! chassons cette importune idée.
   Kabale und Liebe, III, i: *Wurm.* "Der Herr Major ist in der Eifersucht schrecklich," and in III, 4 he is made to appear so before Wurm's plot has begun to work.

[5] *Dialekt- und Ausländer-typen* (1911, p. 174.) He offers no evidence.

sors Brandl and Bradley content themselves with saying that Othello's is not the ordinary sort. To deny that he is jealous in the end (whatever he was at first) is, as Wetz says, mere word-splitting. Coleridge's difficulty lay, however, not in the word or in the passion as here we have it, but, without his being aware, in the convention, which, amid his philosophical prepossessions, he could not comprehend. He insists on the "predisposition to suspicion" (which in Othello, he rightly declares, is wanting) as essential;[1] and yet does not see that, in the temptation scene and after, he is an altered, a different man, suspicious as a Turk. As such, he quite fills the bill of jealousy as drawn up—to prove that he did not fill it—by Coleridge himself:

1. "An eagerness to snatch at proofs."—As in the case of the dream and the handkerchief as well as in his intent and gaping wonder (of which we presently speak) at Iago's mysterious allusions in the beginning. When the dream is told Othello cries out at once, "O monstrous! monstrous!" as if he had never dreamed or been lied to before. Iago faint-heartedly pooh-poohs the dream, but Othello is quick to answer him:

> But this denoted a foregone conclusion;
> 'Tis a shrewd doubt, though it be but a dream.

And when he hears of the handkerchief he is at once for blood.

> If it be that—
> O that the slave had forty thousand lives![2]

2. "A grossness of conception and disposition to degrade the object of his passion by sensual fancies and images."—As, in his words, "lie with her and on her," "lips and noses," "goats and monkeys," and we need not further particularize.

3. "Catching occasions to ease the mind by ambiguities, equivoques, by talking to those who cannot, and who are known not to be able to, understand what is said to them."—As in his remarks about the pain in his forehead, and the handkerchief being too little, and in the various flings and innuendoes by which he carries out the fiction of his visit to Desdemona's bed-chamber as to a house of ill fame, Emilia being the bawd.

4. "A dread of vulgar ridicule."—As in his continual allusions to his being cuckolded, "a fixed figure for the time of scorn to point his slow unmoving finger at."

5. And "a spirit of selfish vindictiveness."—As in the outcries for blood, his vows to tear her to pieces, to chop her into messes, and to throw Cassio's nose to the dogs.

The only other characteristics indicated by Coleridge (besides, of course, the predisposition) are the "solitary moodiness" and the "confused, broken, and fragmentary manner" of dialogue. As for this last, a jerky or spasmodic utterance is peculiar to the Elizabethan comic jealous man—"horn-mad" (generally with the predisposition explicitly indicated) as are Master

---

[1] *Op. cit.*, p. 530, 381; see *ibid.* for the five particulars which follow, and *Cf. Table Talk* (*Works*, Shedd ed. vi, p. 285).

[2] Harris, *The Man Shakespeare*, p. 283: "Othello was surely very quick to suspect Desdemona, he remembers Iago's first suspicious phrase, ponders it and asks its meaning. He is as quick as Posthumus was to believe the worst of Imogen, as quick as Richard II was to suspect his friends Bagot and Greene." etc.

Ford,[1] Kitely in *Every Man in his Humour*,[2] Maybery in *Northward Ho*,[3] and peculiar (in less measure only) to the serious, though hardly tragic, characters Posthumus and Leontes.[4]

So all that Coleridge's distinctions come to is, that Othello, as he himself says, is "not *easily* jealous," and that he is not, in the freaks of his fancy, a vulgar cuckold. Indeed, it is possible that once when he asks for the handkerchief, he, too, shows, like Posthumus and Leontes, something of the comic figure's spasmodic and frantic utterance, comic though he is not.[5] And in every other way he fills the bill, for Coleridge's description above is quite in keeping with the "humour" as exemplified on the Elizabethan stage, or as described by the character-writers or by the classical Burton.[6] Leontes, Ford, and Kitely[7] also snatch at proofs, and Posthumus depends on a strange scoundrel's word and the flimsiest of circumstantial evidence. Quite like Othello, Kitely, when first he meets his wife after his jealousy has been aroused, declares that his "head aches extremely on a sudden," whereupon, like Desdemona, she puts her hand to his head to comfort it;[8] and in his first fit of grief he too cries, "What meant I to marry?"[9] And Posthumus is another who rages for vengeance, would tear his wife to pieces,[10] endeavors to kill her, and, pure-minded as he is before and after, speaks of her—thinks of her—only as a "cunning" courtesan,[11] never considers the possibility of her really loving his rival, and dwells on degrading and bestial thoughts and images.[12] Even by the standard of other plays, then, Othello is jealous, and so he is called throughout the seventeenth century—by Abraham Wright in 1637, as by Sir Charles Sedley in 1693 and George Granville[13] in 1698; and before the undramatic, untheatrical Coleridge, so far as I am aware, no one ever dreamed of his being anything else.

[1] "Fie, fie, fie! Cuckold! cuckold! cuckold!" *Merry Wives*, II ii, 327; "Buck! I would I could wash myself of the buck! Buck, buck, buck! Ay, buck; I warrant you, buck, and of the season, too, it shall appear." III, iii. 167f.

[2] III, ii and iii, *passim*.

[3] Webster's *Works* (1897), vol. i, p. 181, *Maybery's* sixth speech.

[4] *Cymbeline*, II, iv, 105: "O no, no, no! 'tis true": ll. 13, 147-9, *Winter's Tale*, I, ii, 108-111; "Too hot, too hot. But not for joy: not joy": ll. 185-90, 233-4, 267-272; 292-95; 299-300. These ejaculations, quite possibly, were then comical.

[5] "Fetch't, let me see't. Fetch me the handkerchief; my mind misgives . . . The handkerchief! . . . . The handkerchief! . . . . The handkerchief!" Something of the same incoherent repetition appears in his utterances before he swoons, but in both these instances we cannot be certain that Shakespeare had this specific quality of jealousy at the moment in mind.

[6] Burton, *Anatomy* (1845), p. 640: "broken pace," "interrupt, precipitate half turns."

[7] Examples abound, and as Wellbred says, "my very breath hath poison'd him."

[8] *Every Man in his Humour*, II, i; *Othello*, III, iii, 282-90. The situation is so similar that Shakespeare must have borrowed it.

[9] *Every Man in his Humour*, II, iii: "Why did I marry?" *Othello*, III, iii. 242.

[10] *Cymbeline*, II, iv. 147; "O, that I had her here, to tear her limb-meal!" *Othello*, III, iii, 431.

[11] *Cymb.*, II, iv., 128; and the note below; *Othello*, IV, ii, 89.

[12] *Cymb.*, II, v. 15-19. So II, iv, 133; 142-3.

[13] *Shakespeare Allusion-Book*, index, sub *Othello*. The references are too numerous to be repeated here.

Still more decisive proof lies in the explicit utterances of the hero and the other characters. On the subject of their own passions Shakespeare's characters are excellently informed. But it is Othello's last words—

> one not easily jealous, but, being wrought,
> Perplex'd in the extreme—

that we must take, not his rash, classically presumptuous words at the beginning:

> Why, why is this?
> Think'st thou I'd make a life of jealousy,
> To follow still the changes of the moon
> With fresh suspicions? ...
>   ... No, Iago;
> I'll see before I doubt, when I doubt, prove;
> And on the proof, there is no more but this,—
> Away at once with love or jealousy.

For presently (if not already), before this same scene is over, both by thought and by deed he gives himself the lie. As for his conception of the nature of his passion, it is that of the jealous Justiniano in *Westward Ho* (1604):

> Being certain thou art false, sleep, sleep, my brain,
> For doubt was only that which fed my pain;[1]

that of the jealous Gomez in Dryden's *Spanish Friar*, who to the remark, "She is employing her thoughts how to cure you of your jealousy," replies, "Yes, by certainty;"[2] and that of the jealous Mrs. Marwood in Congreve's *Way of the World*:

> Oh! if he should ever discover it he would know the worst and be out of his pain, but I would have him ever to continue upon the rack of fear and jealousy.[3]

And in fact he clamors for proof again and again, more, apparently, because he wishes to ease himself than because he expects to clear his wife;[4] but when, as he thinks, he gets it, then, certainly, he does away with neither love

---

[1] Webster, *Works*, i, p. 72.

[2] *Op. cit.*, IV, i.

[3] II, i. To the same effect Fainall, III, iii: "Jealous of her I cannot be, for I am certain of her guilt; so there's an end of jealousy." This, and the trait mentioned in the text above and the note just below—that of insisting on proof as if guilt were the thing desired—are unmistakably the conventional earmarks of jealousy. They both appear in Strindberg's *The Father*, Act II. "*Captain.* Deliver me from uncertainty, tell me outright that my suspicions are justified, and I will forgive you in advance. *Laura.* You really can't expect me to take upon myself a sin I have not committed. You seem to hope it is true. *Captain.* Yes, strangely enough." For the Elizabethans, no doubt, convention and reality were one and the same. For the analytical Swede the reality may have lain only in the notion (probably better founded) that as long as he was uncertain the jealous man would *think* this state more painful than certainty.

[4] See III, iii, 359-60; 364-7; 390. Cf. my *John Webster*, p. 64.—To be sure, the trait is in the novel of Cintio. "Se non mi fai, disse, vedere, cogli occhi quello, che detto mi hai, viviti sicuro, che ti farò conoscere, che meglio per te sarebbe, che tu fossi nato mutolo." Furness, p. 381.

nor jealousy. The unconscious irony in his words, like that in those of Orosmane,[1] which are conceived, indeed, in imitation of Othello's:—

> Moi jaloux! qu'à ce point ma fierté s'avilisse?—

is a touch repeated in Desdemona's opinion that

> the sun where he was born
> Drew all such humours from him,[2]

which immediately precedes his entrance frantically to demand the handkerchief. "Is not this man jealous?" asks Emilia after he is gone. Desdemona confesses that she had "ne'er seen this before," and they proceed, with interruptions, to discuss the cause of jealousy whether in him or in other men.[3]

Finally, there is a significant parallel pointed out by Mr. Harris between Othello and the jealous Posthumus at the moment when they come from under the slanderer's spell:

"As soon as Posthumus is convinced of his mistake he calls Iachimo 'Italian fiend' and himself 'most credulous fool,' 'egregious murderer,' and so forth. He asks for 'some upright justicer' to punish him as he deserves with 'cord or knife or poison,' nay he will have 'tortures ingenious.' He then praises Imogen as the 'temple of virtue,' and again shouts curses at himself and finally calls upon his love:

> O Imogen!
> My queen, my life, my wife! O Imogen,
> Imogen, Imogen!

Othello behaves in exactly the same way; he calls Iago that 'demi-devil,' and himself 'an honourable murderer' . . . Othello, too, cries for punishment; instead of tortures ingenious he will have 'devils' to 'whip' him, and 'roast him in sulphur.' He praises Desdemona as 'chaste' . . . then curses himself lustily and ends his lament with the words: O Desdemon! dead, Desdemon! dead!"[4]

To Mr. Harris this means, again, that it is only the poet that is speaking; to the historical student of the drama it can mean only that here is another point of likeness between Othello and another jealous hero of the poet's own.

All this does not mean that we deny to Othello's passion that nobler and loftier aspect, first discerned by Coleridge, and best described, perhaps, by Mr. Bradley, who, at the same time, does not fail to recognize the jealousy at the bottom. Our hero grieves at "the wreck of his faith and his love,"[5] at the ravage and havoc there has been

> there where I have garner'd up my heart,
> Where either I must live, or bear no life.

But this thought, like Othello's later notion, worthy of a Spaniard—or of an

---

[1] I, v, 301.

[2] This, as Pellissier (*Shakespeare*, 1914, pp. 165-6) remarks, shows how little of Schlegel's race psychology (see below, p. 46) was in Shakespeare's mind.

[3] III, iv.

[4] Pp. 291-2.

[5] *Shakespearean Tragedy* (1908), p. 194.

Englishman,[1] an Englishman declares,—that the murder is done in a holy cause, and that she must die else she'll betray more men, is not the moving force in the play, is not even, as Mr. Bradley thinks, "the chief or the deepest source of Othello's suffering."[2] A shock to one's faith or idealism is hardly the thing to make one cry out for "blood," thrice over, or to drive one straight to thoughts of mutilation and murder. The passage of two lines just quoted—which Mr. Bradley quotes too—immediately follows one about the ignominy of cuckoldom, and immediately leads to another:—

> or keep it as a cistern for foul toads
> To knot and gender in! Turn thy complexion there,
> Patience, thou young and rose-lipped cherubin,
> Ay, there, look grim as hell.

And there the idealism is far to seek. "Odd that it does not occur to the husband," as Mr. Shaw says of the hero of a modern play, "that if there is poison taken he is the man to take it."[3] Even when, as Desdemona appears, he says, "I'll not believe it," he does not proceed to repent of his suspicions—neither then nor at a later time. His repentance is only for his frightful murderous blunder at the end. It is otherwise with the politer, more modern Orosmane, when reassured:

> Est-ce à moi de me plaindre? on m'aime, c'est assez:
> Il me faut expier par un peu d'indulgence
> De mes transports jaloux l'injurieuse offense.

Othello is, then, jealous—Iago's words, later to be considered,[4] if no others, would settle that,—but is it possible to take it that in the matter of the "predisposition" Desdemona, Iago, Lodovico, and Othello himself, are wrong? If Othello alone had spoken to this intent, and only at the beginning, that might be; but, in accordance with the old superstition, in Shakespeare and the Elizabethan drama generally, the man (not a villain) who is about to pay the debt to nature, speaks by the card. Not that it is a matter of superstition mainly: it is rather a matter of technique. In general we must believe the last words in the tragedy concerning the characters in question,

---

[1] See, for instances the Duke's last long soliloquy in Lope's *El Castigo sin Venganza*. He too thinks himself the minister of heaven.—Mr. Harris (p. 289) says the morality is English.
[2] Bradley, *ibid.*

[3] It is idle to insist that Shakespeare had no choice and that Othello's conduct is in keeping with the "unwritten law" of his age. Othello's morals are stage morals, as are the morals of the revenging, soul-killing Hamlet, or of grand opera with its Senecan tradition of revenge to-day. Heywood wrote *The Woman Killed by Kindness* about 1603, and even a Spaniard—a Lope de Vega—could in those days write:

> Porque la venganza propia
> Para castigar las damas
> Es dejarlas con su gusto.

[4] See below, p. 24.

whether spoken by the hero himself, or by Fortinbras,[1] or by Antony concerning Brutus, remembering that they in some measure take the place of the final choral comment in Greek tragedies or in such Elizabethan ones as *Faustus*. There is no place, to my knowledge, in all Elizabethan tragedy where a hero's final judgment on himself is inexact, still less a judgment ratified by the other principal characters of the play. Besides, the facts are for us: "free and open" Othello is, up to the temptation scene. Not a trace of suspicion, jealousy, or "uneasiness" is to be found in him, any more than in Posthumus before he sees the bracelet in the Italian's hand.

The reason why the predisposition to jealousy is posited by critics such as Gervinus, Wetz, Ulrici, and, indeed, in some form or other, even by many of the orthodox,[2] is, as we have suggested, that without it he cannot, to our modern minds, remain a character at all. Unity, continuity, we crave at any cost. Wetz, by a sophism, an un-Shakespearean, untheatrical refinement,[3] declares him, not already a jealous nature, to be sure, but by temperament and the ticklish circumstances disposed to be that. His trustfulness, strange to say, inclines him to distrust. Admitting that Othello resembles Master Ford in the groundlessness and readiness of his suspicions, Wetz yet finds the main cause of them not in the convention of slander, but in the disparity of rank, color, and years, and in the artificial way in which their love arose. Othello's love was no true passion, as clearly appears from his readiness, unlike Romeo, to sail at once for Cyprus and leave his love behind,[4] and from his ungallant regrets for his former unhousèd, free existence![5] The deepest bliss that he feels does not fill his heart, does no more than silence for the moment his tormenting thoughts![6] And for all his cheerful response to Brabantio's warning, doubt and fear are already gnawing away within him![7] This, if in the unfinical Shakespeare it were anything, would be not only the predisposition but jealousy itself. So, like

---

[1] Professor W. F. Trench (*Shakespeare's Hamlet* (1913), p. 238-40), thinks that in Fortinbras's remark at the end, to the effect that Hamlet would have made an excellent king, the poet is "poking fun" at us. And he hears "Shakespeare cry Ha, ha!" This is an example of the ingenious but utterly arbitrary and unscientific criticism which is daily given to the world. No dramatist but a Strindberg could think of doing the like today; no dramatist, of whatever name, could have thought of doing it in Shakespeare's time. It is not merely a matter of mirth misplaced (though in tragedy Shakespeare is careful enough to put away the cap and bells long before anguish and death draw nigh) but it is rather a matter of making his judgment on the hero's character clear. No dramatist of any time, no Strindberg or Wedekind, much less the explicit Shakespeare, would have poked fun after a fashion that no audience, unprovided with the critic's key, could possibly understand.

[2] See, as to Mr. Bradley, below, p. 46.

[3] I cannot undertake to indicate the various degrees of predisposition which the German critics discover. Ulrici may, on the whole, be numbered among the orthodox, and yet he finds the "germs" of Othello's later passion already in his breast.

[4] *Shakespeare vom Standpunkte*, etc. (1890) p. 296.

[5] P. 297. Cf. I, ii, 25-27.

[6] P. 296.

[7] P. 297. Cf., in *Englische Studien*, xxxii, p. 296, Wetz again to the same effect.

Gervinus, Wetz finds, not a device of tragic construction, but a deep though dim misgiving, in the hero's foreboding on the quay:

> I fear
> My soul hath her content so absolute
> That not another comfort like to this
> Succeeds in unknown fate.

And (not unnaturally) the readiness and promptness with which he takes up with innuendo and slander seems to Wetz, Flathe, and others to indicate that Iago is only ancillary, and that the suspicions all lay slumbering deep in the recesses of the Moor's own brain.[1]

Thus (though by what is after all the only possible way of preserving the character's psychological integrity) Gervinus, Wetz, (in some fashion or other) most of the other Germans, and even Englishmen like Mr. Bradley,[2] thwart and contradict the intention of the poet, whether as expressed by the hero's own opinion and that of the principal persons of the play, or as found in the rôle itself. Certainly no one but a philosopher, no playwright, no audience, no Elizabethan scholar, even, who is not bent and intent upon making his point, can find in Othello, untempted, traces of "uneasiness" or "anxiety," "tormenting thoughts," misgivings, or "unsatisfied love." The foreboding of his rapture is the regular thing in Elizabethan tragedy, and no more means anxiety as to the permanence of their love than does Juliet's in the garden. All the inwardness of it amounts to no more than the ingrained superstitious notion of men that good things cannot last. But a particle of truth these more logical psychologists—these more illogical critics—really have. Once Iago begins to ply his arts, Othello has now, though not before, if not the predisposition, at least the disposition, the inclination, call it what you will. Even the orthodox, who insist that he is not jealous by temperament, cannot help implying it nevertheless. "He cannot observe and interpret trifles," says Sir Walter Raleigh; "his way has been to thrust them aside and ignore them." Why not, then, these? Why rage for blood when told about a dream and a handkerchief? "He is impatient of all that is subtle and devious, as if it were a dishonour." Why listen to an insinuating slanderer and set on his wife to watch? "He credits others freely with all his own noblest qualities."[3] And why not then the wife of his bosom?

In truth, he now is uneasy, anxious, jealous—but he is now a different man. Simply reason and the constitution of our minds demand that so we should take it if Othello is really to be a man at all. *Natura non facit saltum*, or at least the Nature that we know. Iago does his thinking for him,

---

[1] Wetz, *op. cit.*, p. 304-5; *Englische Studien, ibid.*

[2] See below, p. 46.

[3] *Shakespeare*, p. 204. Cf. the similar psychology of Dowden, *Mind and Art* (N. Y. 1901), p. 209, and below, p. 33. At p. 197 the eminent critic first quoted insists—and rightly, of course, if he meant only before the temptation begins—that the Moor is not a jealous man.

Iago puts jealousy upon him, and that our human, hardheaded imaginations cannot conceive or compass, save on the supposition that (though of a sudden) the jealous disposition is already within him, and judgment fled to brutish beasts. In a moment he

> whose solid virtue
> The shot of accident nor dart of chance
> Could neither graze nor pierce,

cries,

> By heaven, he echoes me,
> As if there were some monster in his thought,

and is "frighted"[1] and "moved"[2] by a pow-wow of mystery and the bare names of jealousy and cuckoldom. In a moment he is hanging upon the Ancient's lips, his eyes fixed on the baleful mesmeric orbs, on the waving wizard hands, and to every suggestion he responds with little better than a groan or a sob.[3]

But of suggestion or hypnotism Shakespeare knew not a thing, nor does he intend to intimate that Othello is in himself now different at all. The dramatist but leans on the convention of slander and *"diabolical* soliciting" —on the unapparent paradox of the "free and open" nature turning to suspicion, which we presently discuss. These premises given, and by the formula of Elizabethan dramaturgy almost anything may follow. Only, in order to expedite matters, Shakespeare leans hard, and Othello presents little or no resistance to temptation, is eager, excited, is, for all his protestations of faith, won over in a trice. Long ago captious and clumsy Rymer had more than an inkling of this: "a tedious drawling tame Goose, gaping after any paultrey insinuation, labouring to be jealous, and catching at every blown surmize."[5] And Robert Gould[6] was there before him:

> How cunningly the Villain weaves his sin,
> And how the other takes the Poison in.

> Et je vois sa raison,
> D'une audience avide, avaler ce poison,[7]

[1] III, iii, 120.

[2] III, iii, 217.

[3] Wolff (ii, p. 180) finds that later in the scene when Iago is producing his "proofs," Othello "saugt gierig sie auf;" but at this point says, "Er sträubt sich das gebotene Gift anzunehmen." To me a careful reading of the text seems to show that at once he is on tenterhooks and all agog. See below, pp. 21-22.

[4] On this very anachronistic suggestion of Lombroso's and Professor Kohler's I have touched in my article "Criminals," etc. (cited above), pp. 74-5.

[5] *Tragedies of the Last Age* (1692), Part ii, p. 120. For further evidence of the truth of the observation see below, pp. 20-22, 25. One who, even once, cites the opinion of the "worst critic who ever lived" has to be on the defensive, yet he can find refuge enough behind the name and example of critics who are neither tyros nor Zoili—Dryden and Mr. P. E. More (see article in *Nation* quoted below, p. 51). Surely the editor of the *Fœdera* was not altogether an ass; as opinion is not condemned simply by the fact that he held it.

[6] The *Playhouse* (1685), see *Allusion-Book*, ii. p. 296.

[7] *Dom Garcie*, II, i.

says the villain who practices upon the peace and quiet of Dom Garcie, who, however, is expressly declared to be, and represented as, jealous by nature and instinct.[1]

> Et m'en remercier comme d'une victoire
> Qui combleroit ses jours de bonheur et de gloire,

he continues; and at this point both villains and victims are respectively alike, as when Othello cries, "I am bound to thee forever," thus thanking his man "for making him egregiously an ass," that it might be fulfilled which had been spoken by Iago the prophet.[2] Though Shakespeare, then, in his absorption in the immediate situation and his disregard for possible inferences or for mere psychological processes, did not so intend it, Othello, becoming jealous, brutal, sensual, so speedily—not to say eagerly—cannot, for all the tempting he undergoes, but seem to us as wrenched and altered at that moment, or else jealous, brutal, sensual, deep down in his heart before. The latter alternative, we have already learned, a just and faithful interpreter cannot possibly entertain.

Altered, like Posthumus, the only difference being in the fact that to the avowed conviction Othello is brought more gradually (though rapidly), by steps and stages, and not without some few momentary revulsions. Posthumus changes not only at once but as a whole.[3] Not jealous by temperament —up to that moment convinced of Imogen's purity—once he lays eyes on the bracelet he is of a sudden horn-mad.[4] He has a bracelet for a handkerchief, and the word of a stranger for that of an "honest fellow"; but by the board in a moment goes all his former self, every vestige of tenderness for his wife, his dignity, purity, and nobility of soul, and his innate aversion to crime. And until he hears of his wife's death he is a raging, cursing cuckold and speaks the language of the Elizabethan jealous "humour." Like Othello, before the scene is over he is for tearing her limb-meal,[5] and quite as Othello threatens to kill Iago if he does not "prove his love a whore,"[6] Posthumus threatens to kill Iachimo if he denies that he has made him a cuckold.[7] But in the case of Othello the change, being less abrupt, lies rather

---

[1] See II, i:—"la pente qu'a le prince à de jaloux soupçons."

[2] II, i, 318.

[3] *Pellissier*, pp. 17-18. Leontes is a case somewhat similar. As M. Pellissier observes, there is no evidence that Leontes is testing Hermione and Polixenes as he presses the king to prolong his visit, and his wife to second him in the suit; and yet when she obeys him he bursts at once into a deadly jealousy, though, so far as we are informed, he had never shown the trait before. Like that of Posthumus, moreover (see below, pp. 54-5), his conversion is complete.

[4] It may be admitted, to be sure, that some few of the speeches preceding betray the fact that he is weakening and merely putting on a brave front; but that would make the change, if less abrupt, little less improbable.

[5] *Cymbeline*, II, iv., 147.

[6] Cf., above, p. 12, note, where in the *novella* Othello threatens to cut out the Ancient's tongue.

[7] *Cymbeline*, II, iv, 145; *Othello*, III, iii, 358-63. So Leontes calls Camillo a liar when Camillo contradicts his opinion concerning Hermione, and "hates" him for it. *W. T.*, I, ii, 300.

in the dispostion to lend an ear to slander, and involves the loss of his god-like calm, his dignity and sense of propriety, his judgment and his wits, only in so far as they might interfere with the change. He is not at once jealous or furious, he has not yet lost his tenderness for his wife. It is such a change as in the swift movement of the stage is not so easily noticed, prob-ably was not noticed by the dramatist himself.

So far as disposition, then, is concerned, the more logical psychologists are right, but the disposition is in a different man. Really Coleridge and the orthodox have the best of it—Othello is untainted, and yet is overwhelmed, at his only vulnerable point, his trustfulness, by superhuman art. Whether aware of the change and the new disposition or not, Shakespeare did not intend that Othello was predisposed, or was dull and gullible, or was blinded by passion or fate. But he attempted the impossible—or perhaps he did all that he intended to do, careless of the contradictions into which, almost un-avoidably, he fell. At all events, he undertook (as the orthodox, equally careless, maintain) to present a noble, trustful soul who is brought to ruin even by his virtues, but whose faith and trust, when the hour of his trial is come, turn out to be laid only on his base and backbiting officer, not on his dear wife and friend.[1] Thus the virtues by which he ruins and is ruined are strange and dubious ones, and he turns out to be not trustful at all, alas! but credulous and suspicious.

In maintaining their position that the very innocence and nobility of Othello's soul and the consummateness of Iago's fraud made it impossible for him to think that Iago could be deceiving him[2] (but made it possible that he should think it of Cassio and Desdemona instead) the orthodox seem to be disregarding the very things which above all they prize—ethics and psy-chology, if logic not so much. A trust in a subordinate which immediately bears fruit in murderous distrust of wife and friend, an inclination to think not good but evil, a love which surrenders to calumny and embraces it, knows no difference between the claims of "honest" acquaintance and those of the dearest one has in the world, and is in utter darkness as to the char-

---

[1] So, as M. Pellissier (p. 234), remarks, Posthumus trusts Iachimo and Imogen's attendants (who would not, he thinks, have even stolen the bracelet for Iachimo) rather than his wife. " 'Oui, songe-t-il, c'est très juste;' et il redemande sa bague. Mais Iachimo prend les dieux à témoin, et, dès lors, le benêt ne conserve aucun doute. 'Les suivantes ont juré fidélité et sont honorables; elles, les corrompre! et un étranger! Non, il l'a possédée.' Ainsi donc, Posthumus se fie plus aux femmes d'Imogène qu'à Imogène elle-même. Rendant la bague," etc.

[2] Bradley (p. 192) says that Othello does think of it and suspects him (cf. the question below, p. 24, wherein he seems, ironically, to be given a glimpse of the truth). But how momentary, ineffective, and negligible that suspicion is, appears from the fact that the sum and substance of his psychology (pp. 189, 191), like that of most English critics (cf. above, p. 4), as well as of Germans such as Vischer and Wolff, is that our hero falls because of his trustfulness, is incapable of distrusting anybody (save his wife), the play being *ebensogut die Tragödie des Ver-trauens als der Eifersucht* (Wolff, ii, 164). Really Othello never suspects Iago, thinks only for an instant of the possibility of his 'slandering her,' and does not trust his wife even when he says "I'll not believe it," but feels his aching forehead.

acter of either,—what virtues, what trust and love, are these?[1] Even "stupidity" (a suggestion which despoils the hero of his tragic dignity and state), will not save the character of one who knows not right from wrong, a devil from an angel of light.

> Avez-vous de son coeur si peu de connaissance?
> Discernez-vous si mal le crime et l'innocence?

cries Racine's Aricie, much to the point, to her lover's father, though not, of course, before the curse has been uttered and heard. So in rounder, less delicate terms Emilia reproaches the Moor, and the Moor reproaches himself, though not one instant before the worst comes to the worst and the lady herself lies dead. But the critics undertake psychologically to explain and defend what happens (luckily unexplained and undefended) only in old plays or old stories—that, like Theseus, Potiphar, or Prœtus, a man should believe, in the hour of destiny, what slanders he is told. The *other* old plays and stories, indeed, are less improbable; for Potiphar or Prœtus trusts his wife rather than his son, whereas Othello, giving only the stranger a hearing, trusts the stranger rather than both wife and friend.

On the strength of the convention, to be sure—that arbitrary but traditional fundamental premise—Iago is quite equal to carrying it off; but on the plain basis of human nature, or of psychology, the feints and insinuations of "that demi-devil" or the devil himself (for at bottom the convention or superstition is nearly the same) would have been wasted, had Othello not been Iago's already and been delivered into his hands. He harkens unto Iago, Iago's counsel seems good in his eyes. Yet, if we know ourselves, the entrenchments of character and personality are not all so lightly leaped over, and the simplest body could long have baffled a more cunning fiend.[2] If Iago's treachery was unthinkable, "unimaginable,"[3] Othello might at least have thought—by the Ancient himself it is suggested—that his prying, jealous disposition had been mistaken. Or he might simply have said to him, putting an end to the tragedy in Act Three, "Sir, this is my wife!" and he

> et d'autres, sur ce gage,
> Auroient du monde entier bravé le témoignage.

[1] How thoroughly it is all a matter of convention and situation-making (not, as I shall no doubt be bidden to remember, of Elizabethan character) appears clearly enough when the Friar (*Much Ado*, IV, i, 160-72) defends Hero against her father simply on the strength of his perception of her purity; or when Heywood, in *The Woman Killed by Kindness*, lets the free and open Frankford say, though he has just heard a true story and a far truer-seeming one than Othello:
> Shall I trust
> The bare report of this suspicious groom,
> Before the double-gilt, the well-hatch'd ore
> Of their two hearts? No, I will lose these thoughts, etc.

That is the way, Shakespeare (as well as Heywood) knows perfectly well, a really loyal, unsuspicious friend and husband would take it, if only he were in the flesh, not in a play.

[2] See below, pp. 33, 38.

[3] See below, p. 33.

It is only upon the presumption, then, that Othello is not a personality, not a psychological entity—unless, indeed, a sadly gullible, jealous one—but a *tabula rasa,* or, changing the figure, clay in the potter's hands, that Iago's arts may prosper and prevail. But these, though extraordinary, are as Wetz, Mr. Brooke, M. Pellissier, and others have shown, far from super-human, are by no means without defect. Particularly is this the case in the first two hundred and fifty lines of the temptation scene, where the villain produces even no such "proof" as (after Othello's return) the dream or the handkerchief, but merely raises a cloud of suspicion about Desdemona and Cassio as he "steals" away. As Flathe and Wetz observe, why should he not steal away, being degraded and disgraced? His friend Othello—he might be "stupid" and still do it—should think of this at once, and should suspect—he might be generous and still do it—the generosity of Iago. And Desdemona's prompt and frank petition on his behalf ought of itself to make clear for what he had come. How questionable, moreover, are the aspersions now cast upon Othello's dearest friend's honor and the part he bore in Othello's courtship, proceeding out of the mouth of the man who had just supplanted him in the lieutenancy—whose testimony had been the cause of his supplanting![1]   Then on the heels of that come the echoes, "shrugs," feints, and dodges, the charges which he makes and unmakes, the hints and secrets which he whisks under his general's nose and sticks in his pocket, the sibylline allusions to cuckoldom and admonitions against jealous rage. Wonderfully clever in itself it all is, and much better handled than in Dolce's *Marianna,* whence it was taken,[2] but from the merely human, the "psycholog-ical," standpoint how utterly misplaced! Again is implied (as unhappily is the case) that Othello had already signed his soul away. For to a man in his senses, let alone a famous general and viceroy, nothing could appear more presumptuous or impertinent. Who has constituted Iago, from the very outset, guardian of Othello's mind and keeper of his conscience? Nor could any conduct seem more unbefitting for a really "honest" friend. He is con-tinually trying to cover up his tracks, he is every moment ready to retreat. An honest man who undertakes to tell you that your wife and your dearest friend have played you false makes a clean breast of it, I suppose, without flourish or ado. He does not twist and turn, tease and tantalize, furtively cast forth the slime of slander and ostentatiously lick it up again. Nor when you ask him what he is driving at does he purse his lips, pat you on the

---

[1] In *Marianna* (Act II) Herod is reasonable enough himself to raise the question of a conspiracy and to bethink him of Salome's hatred as the efficient cause of the Cup-bearer's maligning the queen. That Othello does not think of Iago's grudge would mean either that he is jealous by nature or is a blockhead—if we forgot that for him to think of it would thwart the poet's pur-pose.

[2] Cf. Ward, ii, p. 169; Klein, v, p. 385. The same method, in little, is used by Sbrigani in Molière's *Pourceaugnac,* II, iv, and Shakespeare may have got it from a French or an Italian source, translated or untranslated. Dolce's *Giocasta* had long been known in an English dress. Ford's D'Avolos, in *Love's Sacrifice,* for the moment another Iago, is done in imitation of Shakespeare's.

shoulder, and say: It were not for your quiet nor your good. Never mind me: I am an uncleanly prying devil! Good name is to be kept at all hazards, and jealousy is the green-eyed monster which doth mock the meat on which it feeds. Good heaven, the souls of all my tribe defend from jealousy! At best a tale-bearer's business is but a questionable one, but it is all the more questionable and suspicious when he has nothing of a tale to tell.[1]

And instead of following him with bated breath and all agape with fear or crying, "By Heaven, he echoes me"—"Ha!"—"O misery!" a man not quite out of his senses might well have taken our Ancient, as La Bruyère thinks his dupes ought to have taken Tartuffe, simply for the double-dealing viper that he is. Rather, he should have struck him, as at Aleppo once he did the turban'd Turk. Can he better brook the "traducing" of his wife and friend than of Venice?[2] Indeed, the nearest Iago at this first session approaches to proof is but to insult his general beyond all bounds. "She did deceive her father," or, as we innocently say, eloped, and not with one "of her own clime, complexion, and degree," but—

> Foh! one may smell in such a will most rank,
> Foul disproportions, thoughts unnatural—

with a Moor! The most pigeon-livered, chicken-hearted creature in the world, we must think, would not have put up with the like of this; and it is doing Shakespeare and his Iago little honor to maintain either that arts such as these are "superhuman," or that the Othello of the Council-chamber has not now vanished from our view.

Not that time and again Iago does not play the honest man in nearly all his honesty, as in the speech:

> Touch me not so near.
> I had rather have this tongue cut from my mouth
> Than it should do offense to Michael Cassio;
> . . . .
> But men are men; the best sometimes forget, etc.

---

[1] A friend and colleague suggests that I underestimate the power of calumny, and he reminds me of Bazile's words on the subject in the *Barbier de Séville* (II, viii). But this is the gossip which floats about and infects the air, and crushes the victim without ever reaching her ears, perhaps, or theirs who love her. A very different thing is this personal slander—without a pretence to evidence or the dear friend's privilege to speak—which, however indirect and clever it be, is, save to a pasha or a Bluebeard, in itself an affront, a violation of the precincts of personality, an alarm to suspicions farthest from its thought to arouse. Besides, as I have shown, this convention of believing the things that you are told works equally well when a character like Malcolm or Dekker's Infelice defames himself; or when, as I show below, p. 26, the process reversed, the calumniator, so implicitly credited, is discredited again by the testimony of a witness whom, before, the hero could not hear, as one corrupted and prejudiced, but who now may be supposed to be more prejudiced than ever. (To be sure, Emilia may be supposed by Othello to have no reason falsely to accuse her husband, but the wife of Iago could have had no reason but the best for contradicting the slanderous report when Othello first repeats it to her, or for cursing the wretch who put the notion into Othello's head. Why had Iago kept his suspicions from Emilia? And why does not Othello see to it that his two contradictory witnesses are in his presence brought face to face?)

[2] V, ii, 351-4:—"beat a Venetian and traduced the State," etc.

But in the scene of which we have been speaking Shakespeare, in his neglect of plausibility, would have us labor, with Othello, under the delusion that the manners of honesty and dishonesty are almost one and the same :[1]

> these stops of thine fright me the more;
> For such things in a false disloyal knave
> Are tricks of custom; but in a man that's just
> They're close delations, working from the heart
> That passion cannot rule;—

a delusion under which he would have us labor *without* Othello when Desdemona's innocence and purity is made to appear, not in its native dauntlessness, but in the guise of timorous and senseless double-dealing.[2] "Utterly trustful," "simple as a saint," says Sir Walter Raleigh (who seems unwilling to defeat the poet's expectations), regardless of the way she lies about the handkerchief and dodges further question, cries "betrayed," "undone," and like a guilty thing weeps and pleads for life! Still, Voltaire and Schiller, it must not be forgotten, expected of us in this kind almost as much.

The unplausibleness of all this manoeuvring of Iago's is abated only as we fall back upon the convention and fundamental premise. Psychologically, Iago's toils are, now or afterward, not at all so ineluctable as Coleridge, Schlegel, Ulrici, Hudson, and the rest of the orthodox think; and possibly Shakespeare himself would have been as much surprised as we at their taking it that any man in Othello's position would have been like him enmeshed.[3] What Othello calls proof (but Iago himself "trifles light as air") comes later; and all that Iago is now doing is, without proof or evidence, as it were by a spell or mesmeric manipulation, to get the man under control, to make the man his own. Othello is changed and jealous, we have seen, at the moment of temptation; but—according to the orthodox criticism as a psychological fact, according to Shakespeare himself, I think, as but a fact in the story—it is Iago himself that changes him. The readiness with which he yields to the process must simply be granted the poet. As we have traced this, it consists in injecting the "medicine," the "poison," as Iago calls it, and then letting it "work," and turn into "proof" evidence however trivial.

> I will in Cassio's lodging lose this napkin,

he says in the moments when Othello is off the stage,

---

[1] See above, p. 6, note 3.

[2] It has been urged that innocent women and children have recourse to deceit from fear. But Desdemona was brave enough, and trustful enough, in running away with the noble black man and in pleading her friend Cassio's suit; and even a timid innocence does not look altogether like guilt. Our discussion of a similar situation in other dramatists above (pp. 6-8) shows how for the situation's sake they have tampered with the integrity of the character.

[3] Cf. Furness, pp. 432, 434, for the two German critics. Cf. Ulrici cited in Wetz, pp. 375-6, and below, p. 49.

> And let him find it. Trifles light as air
> Are to the jealous confirmations strong
> As proofs of holy writ: this may do something.
> The Moor already changes with my poison.
>
> III, iii, 321f.

So later he says:

> And his unbookish jealousy must construe
> Poor Cassio's smiles, gestures, and light behaviours
> Quite in the wrong.
>
> IV, i, 103

At bottom is the notion, expressed in the play repeatedly and in all **Eliz-abethan** literature as well, that, as Emilia says, jealous souls

> are not ever jealous for the cause
> But jealous for they're jealous. It is a monster
> Begot upon itself, born on itself.
>
> III, iv, 159f.

But Iago's own words make his method clear—to "put the Moor into a jeal-ousy so strong that judgment cannot cure," and then, merely suggesting, never convincing, let passion run its course. And this he does as if the Moor were an hypnotic subject or a brainless beast, by repeating the words "good name," "jealousy," and "cuckold," almost as if he were crying "sick 'im" to a dog. No man not jealous by nature was ever thus put into a jealousy without process of proof or show of reason; no man's soul ever thus lay in the hollow of another's hand.

The passage quoted above—"These stops of thine fright me the more"— is one of those which might favor a theory of *tragische Verblendung*, though I do not know that it has been used. Now, perhaps, and afterward—"if thou dost slander her and torture me, never pray more"—the hero is, iron-ically, given a glimpse of the truth that he cannot really see. This is a characteristically Shakespearean device, as is its counterpart, Othello's out-cry "Who can control his fate?" at the end. But what the Germans say, is, that the action of Fate is the pervading idea, and the cause of Othello's downfall. "The hero were a fool, if he had to do only with an Iago," says Professor Brandl, "and behind Iago stands a perverted world-order, which he serves."[1] And thereby the critic betrays, on the one hand, a fitting dis-content with the story of the slanderer believed as an image of life (though failing to recognize its impermanent warrant in convention), and, on the other hand, the philosophical bias (soon to be noticed) which turns coinci-dences and lack of motivation in a play into an intentional representation of what happens in the world.

The commoner German interpretation, as that of Wetz[2] and Vischer, is

---

[1] *Shakespeare*, pp. 161-2.
[2] P. 301.

that the Moor is blinded by his passions. And so flimsy is Iago's evidence, so considerable should be Othello's prejudice against it when produced, that, if everything in a play must be reduced to terms of character, for some theory or other of blindness there is, in all conscience, justification enough. He takes up at once, we have seen, with Iago's insinuations, resenting none of his impertinence, remembering nothing of Cassio's friendship and Desdemona's purity and love. For a time Iago simply plays with the Moor's imagination, as he touches upon jealousy and cuckoldom, the falseness of Venetian women, his wife's deception of her father,[1] and the unequal and unnatural union, flaunting these inflammatory images before his eyes as the bull-fighter does his cloak. And when he comes to proof—still he flaunts infuriating images by the way, as the vision of Desdemona in Cassio's embraces, Cassio's movements in his dream, and his use of the precious handkerchief to wipe his beard. Proof and this tale of a dream and a handkerchief have nothing in the world in common, and yet all Othello can do is to cry, not fiddlededee! but "monstrous, monstrous!"—"O that the slave had forty thousand lives," and swear to heaven his revenge. In the next scene and the first of Act IV it would appear that to Desdemona and Othello, as to the finical Ulrici, the loss of a lady's handkerchief is almost tantamount to the loss of her good name, though nothing is easier to lose or steal unless it be a hairpin or an umbrella. Desdemona deplores the loss of her "napkin" before Othello enters, and acknowledges that it were enough to put him to ill-thinking;[2] and after he enters, though he is already convinced of her adultery, he himself has nothing to ask but that he may set eyes on it, and he will talk of nothing else.

In Act IV Iago resumes his play on the imagination, ironically calling up visions of kissing, being naked in bed together, and things more bestial still, before his ensanguined eyes. Then comes the swoon, and then the overhearing of Cassio. By this time, to be sure, the maddened mind of the Moor

---

[1] "And so she did," replies Othello; and much has been made of this as well as of Brabantio's final warning. Shakespeare might have made much more of it himself, for Othello never recalls the warning, never reverts to these words of Iago's. But whatever he made of it, one cannot, with Ulrici, speak of Iago's as an *Argument von grosser Probabilität*. Does a man distrust the woman who elopes with him, or would he entertain such a thought when suggested by a friend? The only importance it can have lies in the effect of it upon a mind naturally suspicious, already alarmed and aroused.

[2] This anticipation is designed, no doubt, both to arouse suspense and to lend plausibility to an unplausible situation. Throughout the play the handkerchief roughly corresponds to Seneca's and Racine's device of the sword of Hippolytus, which Phædra, or her Nurse, like Potiphar's wife with Joseph's garment in her hand, uses as circumstantial evidence. The abandoned garment or sword certainly shows that something desperate has happened, but the handkerchief shows nothing at all.

A friend of mine urges, with the commentators, that it was no ordinary handkerchief; but we do not discover that, nor does Desdemona, till Othello tells of its magical qualities after it has been lost (III, iv, 55-68). This, it would seem, is a tale made up for the occasion to scare the poor lady into betraying her guilt. In no way does it make more plausible Othello's thinking her guilty simply because of the fact that Cassio holds in his hand a thing of hers so easily lost, the value of which she had not known.

is quite ready to be imposed upon, but still the grossness of the imposition is almost beyond belief. If the possession of a lady's handkerchief is proof of adultery with her, how preposterous that Cassio, now pleading for his favor, should be wiping his beard with it in public or unconcernedly producing it before Iago or his drab! And only less preposterous is Othello's mistaking of Cassio's report of the "customer" Bianca's haunting him and publicly falling him about the neck, for a report concerning the daughter of the Magnifico, gentle Desdemona.[1] Throughout his jealousy, however, like Posthumus, as we have seen, Leontes, and all other jealous Elizabethan heroes, noble though they be, he never considers the possibility of her falling in love with the man, or the possibility of Cassio's surpassing him in personal charm or in wit, but takes her only for a "cunning" and "delicate" courtesan, without a heart, without the right to love and choose.

All this, I say, together with the arbitrary hardening of Othello's heart against Emilia's testimony, like Herod's in Dolce's play against that of Cupbearer or Councillor, Wetz, Flathe, and others call the blinding of passion; Dr. Brandes,[2] Mr. Stopford Brooke, and others, stupidity; Professors Brandl and Bradley,[3] as we have seen, the influence of fate and a perverted world. One and all, however, they marvel, not at Othello's belief, but only at Iago's ineluctable toils. But this conviction, forced upon him—"such a conviction as any man would and must have entertained"—is put off almost as lightly as it was put on. Now that on the stage (though not at all in the mind of Othello) the time is ripe and fully come, Emilia's assertion that often Iago had begged her to steal the handkerchief has weight which was wanting to all her previous solemn protestations of Desdemona's innocence, and he runs at the miscreant with drawn sword. In a trice she is cleared,[4] as in a trice she was incriminated, and by Iago's stealing the handkerchief as by Cassio's once having it in his hand. It is a poor rule that works only one way, disbelief ought to be as easy as belief[5]—but if ever psychology did not matter it is here. In the last analysis, the slanderer was believed that there might be a story, and the slanderer is now repudiated that the story may end.[6]

"Blindness," stupidity," inevitable "conviction"—mere convention is all

---

[1] This point and that in the preceding sentence are made by Wetz. There is the further unplausibility, noted by others, in Iago's suspicious demeanor—speaking low one moment and loud the next. But that is a convention which must be granted as generously as the aside. As a matter of mere fact, to be sure, the actor Othello hears all the audience hears.

[2] *Shakespeare* (1909), p. 443.

[3] See also below, p. 27.

[4] See V, ii, 220-235.

[5] As a matter of fact it is generally more difficult, and that Shakespeare should make the process so much quicker and easier, in Leontes and Posthumus as well as Othello, shows either how little he knew of the psychology of the matter or how little he regarded it.

[6] Cf. my article "Criminals," p. 75.

that I can make of it, or else what Bulthaupt[1] makes of it, unplausibility, improbability in the arrangement of the play. There is not a tragedy of intrigue and slander in the world without similar defects, and the hero is not "blinded" but sees only what for the purposes of a tragic plot the poet vouchsafes him to see. A pretty trick of the apologist it is to turn all these inconsequences in the action into traits of the hero as a man! Masterpieces, at that rate, would be thick as blackberries and every scribbler no less than a "bard." At bottom it is the same confusion of art and life as in Mr. Brooke's and Professor Bradley's and others' transformation into Fate or Chance of all the coincidences which fill up for Iago the gaps in his intrigue. To these we now for a few moments turn.

"Again and again," says Mr. Bradley of Iago, "a chance word from Desdemona, a chance meeting of Othello and Cassio, a question which starts to our lips and which anyone but Othello would have asked, would have destroyed his life. In their stead Desdemona drops her handkerchief at the moment most favorable to him,[2] Cassio blunders into the presence of Othello only to find him in a swoon, Bianca arrives precisely when she is wanted to complete Othello's deception and increase his anger into fury." Besides those improbabilities enumerated by Mr. Brooke below, Mr. Bradley might also have mentioned: Othello's patiently waiting, for all his fury, instead of bursting out on Cassio then and there;[3] Iago's trusting the key to his character, his plans, and his fate, to a tool-villain so "loose of soul" as Roderigo,[4] who is just the man to peach; his begging Emilia, on an earlier occasion, to steal the handkerchief and his now snatching it from her, though all that she says about it later she might equally well have said in time; and his contriving the quarrel with Cassio before he knows that Cassio will look to the guard,[5] apparently, indeed, without knowledge of his "poor and unhappy brains for drinking"[6] and his quarrelsomeness when drunk. As for the handkerchief, in a footnote Mr. Bradley adds: "And neither she nor

---

[1] Frequently he too speaks of the stupidity of the characters, as on pp. 210-12, and when he declares that if the other characters had had a grain of his wit Iago could not have succeeded in his plans. But at these moments he seems to be using the language of men rather than of critics, for at other times he dwells on the lack of motivation and the intrusion of coincidence.

[2] This element of chance is less prominent, as has been observed, in the novel of Cintio. There Iago deliberately steals it.

[3] Noticed by Bulthaupt, pp. 221-2. Salvini (Furness, p. 237), who omitted this portion of the scene (as much as IV, i, 50-194) says, "Should you not suppose that he would spring like a tiger on Cassio and tear him to pieces?" And such opinion far outweighs that of Wetz, p. 340, who opposes it. It is highly unplausible that Othello should have been so easily imposed upon, but being so imposed upon, he would not have been held in leash merely by Iago's general injunction to be "patient." If he had been patient and reasonable enough for that, he might have been patient and reasonable enough to consider and question the evidence—patient and reasonable enough to come forth from covert, confront Cassio, and hear what he has to say.

[4] This is an established Elizabethan convention, of course, which provided opportunity for comic diabolical confabulations between rogue and rogue.

[5] II, iii, 1. Cf. II, i, 270 ff.

[6] II, iii, 40.

Othello observes what handkerchief it is. Else she would have remembered how she came to lose it, and would have told Othello: and Othello, too, would at once have detected Iago's lie that he had seen Cassio wipe his beard with the handkerchief 'today.' For in fact the handkerchief had been lost not an hour before Iago told that lie (line 288 of the same scene) and it was at that moment in his pocket. He lied therefore most rashly, but with his usual luck."

Luck! One would think the stage were Cyprus itself, and Iago not a bundle of words in verse and prose but flesh, blood, and bone. By the standards of art, by the limitations or opportunities with which he was confronted, our dramatist must be judged like any other mortal artist, and not be given a patent to offend. But by dint of mere assertion Mr. Brooke, Mr Bradley and others turn all these defects into virtues, as if he were not so much an artist as the supreme Artificer, and whatever is were right or so must be. "All this and much more seems to us quite natural," continues Mr Bradley after the recital of the instances of Iago's "good fortune," quoted above, "so potent is the art of the dramatist: but it confounds us with a feeling such as we experience in the *Œdipus Tyrannus,* that for those star-crossed mortals—both *dusdaimones*—there is no escape from fate,[1] and even with a feeling, absent from that play, that fate has taken sides with villainy."

This is evidently something such as Professor Brandl means, but as long as this method prevails with it Shakespeare criticism will remain a contradiction in terms. Justly enough, Mr. Brooke dwells upon the "blind unreasonable chance" and improbability in Othello's, Emilia's, and everybody else's ignorance of the monster's character, in a wise and cautious general's so stupidly succumbing to him, in his failure to feel Desdemona's innocence intuitively, to make inquiry concerning the handkerchief, or to discredit the notion that Cassio would give away the token to his drab.[3] But all this "shocking unreasonableness," shows, he says, "the power of baleful Chance in the world, not chance in [the poet's] work. . . . He combined all the improbabilities with so creative and formative an imagination that the whole play seems eminently probable. We are hurried on so fast from the first suspicion of Othello to his death that we have no time to ask questions, to doubt or debate anything."[4]

Quite the same may be said of many a melodrama that gets short shrift from the critics today, and would get shorter from Mr. Brooke, I judge. But what double-tongued, damning praise! He combined and hurried over all the improbabilities! These are defects, then, these bits of

---

[1] As to Fate in Shakespeare, see below, pp. 30-31.

[2] P. 182. See below, p. 29, and p. 30, for examples of the same thing taken from Swinburne and Loening.

[3] *Ten More Plays of Shakespeare,* pp. 171 ff.

[4] *Ibid.,* p. 175.

philosophy, glimpses into a "distracted world-order," revelations of a "belief in chance as at the root of the universe," which make the mood of the drama as a whole—and these it is a merit in the poet, after damaging the play by introducing them, to hurry over and conceal! Certainly Mr. Brooke confuses "chance in the world" and "chance in his work" if Shakespeare does not, though with each other the things have nothing to do. It is but the familiar, traditional error of the craft.[1] In a play which shows Chance at the root of the Universe motivation is surely as needful as in a play which shows Necessity. The play must not be a chaos if the world is; the fortuitous must be represented with an art wherein there is nothing fortuitous; and sensible people must not fail, if need be, to remember their handkerchiefs, to use their wits, and to pick up some little knowledge of one another. The want of this in the play indicates, if anything, not Chance in the universe, but an over-ruling Providence in the poet! *Il réussit, dira-t-on,* says of Iago a French critic, free of our pre-possessions, yet admired, to my surprise, by so thorough-going a Shakespearean as Dr. Furness;[2]—*il réussit, ainsi le veut l'auteur.* The dice of Zeus fall ever luckily. And what had then De Broglie to say of the flaws which are merits? "Such are the depth and variety of the first conception that the most striking improbabilities, the most inconceivable absurdities, pass unobserved, because no one has leisure to look to the motives of the action; but to make these absurdities out to be merits is quite another matter." At the theatre we pass them over only because of *other* merits, which abound.[3] And what we have

---

[1] Cf. Swinburne's article on Webster (cited p. 31, below), justly criticized by Mr. Archer. "The fifth act of the *Duchess of Malfi* has been assailed on the very ground which it should have been evident to a thoughtful and capable reader that the writer must have intended to take up—on the ground that the whole upshot of the story is dominated by sheer chance, arranged by mere error, and guided by pure accident" (p. 879). The amazing implication is that in order to represent caprice in Fate or Providence the poet may be capricious himself.

[2] *Op. cit.,* p. 452—Cf. the remarks of Bulthaupt, ii, p. 210 ff: "Aber ein trügerischer Boden, eine halbe, lückenhafte, und gerade an den wichtigsten Stellen völlig aussetzende Motivirung, und die Spekulation auf jene Macht mit der bekanntlich auch die Götter vergebens kämpfen, die aber immer als tragischer Hebel bedenklich ist und bleibt." By the side of such a judgment, from a scholar who knows the drama, ancient and modern, through and through, how trivial, unenlightened appear the criticisms of most of our literary critics! Not that the Germans are our only light. Both Bradley and Brooke have recognized the lack of motivation, though they justify it. Wolff, on the other hand, goes so far as to say (II, 185): "Mit zwingender Nothwendigkeit entwickelt die Handlung sich aus den drei leitenden Charakteren." And Volkelt, *Ästhetik des Tragischen* (1897), p. 153, to the same unhappy effect.

[3] "In the third Act we have peripety handled with consummate theatrical skill. To me—I confess it with bated breath—the *craftsmanship* seems greatly superior to the psychology. Othello, when we look into it, succumbs with incredible facility to Iago's poisoned pinpricks; but no audience dreams of looking into it; and there lies the proof of Shakespeare's technical mastery." Even Mr. Archer (*Playmaking,* p. 202) here seems to lend support to heresy and superstition. But we observe that he says "audience," and is thinking of Shakespeare's undoubted success in attaining his temporary end. (See below, p. 57). Still he comes to what is, as I think, but an illogical conclusion, and technical mastery would be proved only by Othello's succumbing *credibly.* Surely Mr. Archer would himself agree with me that we have had enough of this sort of criticism (though it is not the worst we have had), which points out a score of flaws, improbabilities, conventionalities—and then, behold, the miracle! and there are no flaws at all!

said of Chance applies equally to Professor Brandl's and Professor Bradley's Fate. The words are different, but in critical phrase—written with capital letters—the notions are hardly so. Fate or Fortune, how many critical crimes have been committed in thy name! For the Shakespearean the word is ever at hand to stop the caviller's mouth, if not to stifle his own critical scruples.

The Shakespearean's Fate is robbed of much of its tragic gravity, however, when we see how readily it puts in an appearance to help the poet out. Things fine and precious are difficult, and how much more difficult it would have been to furnish Iago with evidence more credible, and an intrigue independent of Chance, fit to inveigle an Othello who trusts his wife and friend as well as his officer, and has not discontinued the use of his wits![1] Why have an Othello that only by a *deus ex machina* can escape being called a fool, even by the poet's worshippers? It is a device that the poet himself would have been first and foremost to disdain. In this play the references to Fate are only[2] two, and, as in most of the poet's plays, such references are momentary and casual. In no play, perhaps, is Fate by him presented as the active agent, but curse and prophecy alike are fulfilled, through human motives, by the free and willing act of man, though often recognized as a miraculous fulfillment afterward.[3] Brabantio's final warning,[4] Othello's foreboding on the quay, and his outcry "Who can control his fate?" in the bedchamber, are hardly more than bits of constructive and rhetorical furniture, imitated, indirectly, from the classics, and designed to focus interest and lend tragic state and emphasis. Utterances of the moment,[5] they do not strike to the centre; but even if they did, it is the poet's own art and effort, not his artlessness, that must make Fate's hand appear. The nearest he comes to that is at moments such as when he lets Romeo and Macbeth defy the destiny which overtakes them; and he has nothing at all like Eteocles or Cassandra driven to their doom, Grillparzer's Jaromir fascinated by the dagger, or Œdipus fleeing from his fate, fulfilling it, and blindly seeking to know it when fulfilled. However Senecan the sentiments his heroes occasionally utter, the heroes themselves are in action free and responsible

---

[1] Even by many of the respectable and learned it is simply used to explain away difficulties often of their own creation. Professor Loening, in his *Hamlet,* p. 394-5, thinking that the hero resists the mandate to the last, has him, by a dispensation of Fate, avenge his father in spite of himself. And then he holds it up as a marvel and mystery of Art. "Es ist als ob der Dichter mit diesem Plane der Vorsehung das Geheimnis ihrer wunderbaren Wege abgelauscht, als ob er da Unerforschliche erforscht, das Unbegreifliche begriffen hat." One wonders that it is still possible for a great scholar to speak in such a vein, in this age of reason.

[2] See Bartlett, *sub voce;* especially II, i, 195; V, ii, 265. In the other three the word seems to be used in the more prosaic, concrete sense.

[3] Cf. what are in this respect the most classical of his plays, *Richard III* and *Macbeth.*

[4] Gervinus takes it for a curse. See below, p. 44.

[5] Cf. Hamlet's words about fate before the duel, and Gloster's and Kent's in *King Lear.* In such "pious ejaculations," however, the villain has no part or lot. Cf. my article *Criminals,* p. 76.

like all other characters in the Renaissance and in large measure Seneca's own.[1] But the point is that we have no more right to call in Fate to cover up this dramatist's workmanship than we have to do that for a dramatist of today. *The Second Mrs. Tanqueray* is a tragedy, and in common parlance, and quite as truly as at any moment in *Othello*, we should say that there is "irony of Fate" at the moment when Paula, at last about to escape from the shadow of her old life, win her stepdaughter Ellean's love, and be happy, finds that Ellean is in love with a young fellow with whom she had once lived herself. Why then does not a critic arise to call in Fate to obliterate the blemish of this coincidence? And why should such a critic get laughed at—and never the Shakespearean—seeing that comparatively it is but a little thing that is asked of Fate?

To return now to the notion of blinding passion, by it the Germans endeavor to do in the field of internal motivation what Professor Bradley, with his "luck" and "Fate," and Mr. Brooke, with his "Chance," endeavor to do in the external. They justify the ways of the Bard to men. Quite apart from the error of a critical method which proceeds on the assumption that the art of Shakespeare is different from the art of any other,[2] there is here the error of presuming a state of anxiety within Othello's bosom from the beginning, and the still greater error of having him blinded by passion at the moment when first Iago opens his tempter's lips. It is easy enough, we have seen, to believe that by passion Othello is blinded to the gross improbabilities of the imposition Iago puts upon him in the conversation between himself and Cassio; but how at the outset does he come to forget the love of Desdemona, the life-long friendship of Cassio, his good and sufficient reason for stealing away as appears from Desdemona's frank petition for him, and at once succumb, though in unutterable anguish, to the shrugs, suggestions, and glittering eye of Cassio's dispossessor?

If Wetz does not undertake to explain it, another[3] does, though one of the orthodox, on the whole, who see the passion springing up only at Iago's word.

---

[1] Professor Cunliffe's *Influence of Seneca*, p. 31. Concerning Shakespeare and Webster in this connection, however, he quotes (p. 27), from an article of Swinburne's (*Nineteenth Century*, June, 1886, p. 868): "With Shakespeare—and assuredly not with Æschylus—righteousness itself seems subject and subordinate to the masterdom of fate." Certainly that is all contrary to fact, and Swinburne, with Mr. Cunliffe's approval, makes, as I cannot but think, the error of confounding the predestinating hand of Fate with that of the poet, and Chance, with a mere dramatist's accident or coincidence (cf. especially *ibid.*, p. 879). In Æschylus, "nemesis," "the god," and "the daimon" so interfere that we can make little of the responsibility of Clytemnestra, Agamemnon, or Orestes; but Macbeth had thought of the deed before, at the "supernatural soliciting" he leaps to meet his fate, and he has no god to blame. It is of course impossible here to discuss this topic adequately—it requires an article or a book in itself. For Shakespeare as the poet of free-will see B. Siburg, *Schicksal und Willensfreiheit* (1906); Heine on Macbeth in *Mädchen und Frauen* (*Werke, Elster ed.*, Leipzig, v, p. 436); my article on "Criminals," p. 76.

[2] See above, p. 28, and my article *"Falstaff."*

[3] Mr. Edward Rose, *New Shakespeare Society Trans.*, 1880-2, p. 1; quoted by Dr. Furness, p. 428 f., with high approval.

"Othello has a strong and healthy mind and a vivid imagination, but they deal entirely with first impressions, with obvious facts. If he trusts a man he trusts him without the faintest shadow of reserve.[1] Iago's suggestion that Desdemona is false comes upon him like a thunderbolt. He knows the man to be honest, his every word the absolute truth.[2] He is stunned, and his mind accepts specious reasonings, passively and without examination. Yet his love is so intense that he struggles against his own nature and for a time compels himself to think, though not upon the great question whether she is false. He cannot bring his intellect to attack Iago's conclusion and only argues the minor point: Why is she false? But even this effort is too much for him. It is, I have said, against Nature; and Nature, after the struggle has been carried on unceasingly for hours, revenges herself—he falls into a fit. The soliloquy at the end of Othello's first scene with Iago may appear to make rather against my theory: it does not merely repeat one thought, it goes from point to point. The contradiction is only apparent. He is trying to force his mind and it flutters helplessly from one minor point to another; moreover, jealousy is a mean and worrying passion attaching itself to details, not grand and broad like the greatest love, hate or ambition. . . . My theory by the way may help to account for what has always troubled critics—the extraordinary quickness with which Othello's faith in Desdemona yields to Iago's insinuations. Sudden and intense emotion stunts his nature and makes it incapable of resistance."

In the critic's reasoning flaws abound. Such a mind is the reverse of strong and healthy, and so feeble an intellect and overweening an imagination would be strange in any man, and all the stranger in a great general and viceroy, "whom passion could not shake,"—

> whose solid virtue
> The shot of accident nor dart of chance
> Could neither graze nor pierce.[3]

Quite the contrary, we have seen, is the impression he makes in the Council-chamber. Not a ripple is there in his equanimity, for all Brabantio's abuse; and when before that he hears from Iago of the Magnifico's scurvy and provoking terms which prompted the honest fellow to "yerk him here under the ribs," he says, "'Tis better as it is," and no more, in fine preparation for the high carelessness of his reception to his father-in-law's outcries and armed approach:

> Put up your bright swords or the dew will rust them!

Put up your doubts and cavils, Iago, men are not so easily stunned. What woman, even, however frail and inexperienced, was ever thus paralyzed by the mere breath and whisperings of slander, so as to believe her husband false?[4] Desdemona is crushed for a moment by her husband's cruelty

---

[1] Cf. Bradley, p. 191, and many others.

[2] Among the orthodox this bit of "psychology" is constantly reappearing, though it implies both that his trust in Desdemona in the first instance is not absolute (which they would deny) and that he hasn't the brain of a rabbit (which, of course, they would deny as well). Indeed, with these implications we all must have nothing to do, for they are contrary to the tenor of Act 1.

[3] IV, i, 277.

[4] Except, of course, in a play, when a situation is at stake. Imogen, as readily as Posthumus, believes the stranger Iachimo when he reports her lover's infidelity, and disbelieves him again only when he makes his own infamous proposals. *Cymbeline*, I, vi.

and disbelief, but her love and faith go on to the end.   A childish simplicity and implicitness of faith, no doubt, is what Mr. Rose, like many critics, German and English, is supposing; but what child, for all his inexperience of duplicity, would hesitate a moment to give the lie to the man who speaks ill of his parents or his friends?   There is the sophism—that trustfulness precipitates one into suspicion, that, with an Iago at hand, the unsuspicious is just the one to fall utterly a prey[1] to doubts which his heart has never known.   "A man of honest, unimaginative mind,"[2] says Professor Schelling, applying to the similar Posthumus, what, with a different "psychology," had been said by Ulrici and others of Othello, "to whom Iachimo's fabricated proofs appeal, but to whom his dastardly trick is unimaginable."[3]   But Imogen's—Desdemona's—falseness is, then, imaginable!   "Naïveté, a childish ignorance of the world and man," says Dr. Wolff;—"why should his tried and trusted Ancient deceive him?"   But why should Desdemona?   "Othello had no defence against it," says Mr. Brooke of Iago's plot, "because he was entirely incapable of conceiving or understanding anything so ignoble."[4]   If experience—or inexperience—or nobility of soul makes him trust Iago, all the more, then, should the one or the other, and his heart's love into the bargain, make him trust her, who had without stint or limit trusted him.   No doubt proof of the falseness of the loved one might lead a trustful child or man to be suspicious generally; but into suspicion Othello is precipitated, without proof.   And it is only by means of a specious and unreal psychology, as I said, that he is made incapable of distrusting the testimony which his whole nature forbids him to accept, to the point of distrusting the testimony and character of those whom both his nature and their own forbid him to discredit.   "His unquestioning faith in Desdemona is his life,"[5] says Sir Walter Raleigh,—in so far that he immediately forsakes her and turns wholly to Iago!

The "struggles against his own nature" and the "effort" to think I, for one, cannot find in the text.   True it is that Othello does not "attack Iago's conclusion," and argues (if he argues at all) only the minor point: Why is she false?   But there, again, is convention, and Shakespeare's method,

---

[1] Cf., Wolff i, pp. 164, 167; Gervinus, p. 530; and it is at the root of the teaching of the orthodox from Coleridge to Bradley (p. 186) and Raleigh (see below).

[2] The warrant for this, as for many another bit of Shakespearean psychology is simply not to be found in the text.   Like Leontes and Othello Posthumus has, up to his wife's apparent death, an imagination capable of conceiving, not the slanderer's treason indeed, but his wife's, in bestial and preposterous detail.   See above, *passim*.

[3] The fact is, Othello is not, as Ulrici and the others declare, wholly incapable of entertaining the thought.   See, for instance, III, iii, 121-2, 367-72, quoted above.   He does not entertain it for long simply because, on the basis of convention, he must trust Iago; but he can conceive of treason well enough.

[4] Wolff, II, p. 164; Schelling, i, p. 575; Ulrici (Bohn), i, p. 427; Brooke, p. 185.

[5] *Shakespeare* (N. Y., 1907), p. 204.

through and through.   Once the Ancient has spoken, as we have repeatedly observed, Othello, though he says he does, never really doubts Iago, never again believes his wife.   But it is not in the least that he cannot "bring his intellect" to the point, or that it is "against nature."   Must the same be said then of Gloster, in *King Lear,* of Claudio, in *Twelfth Night,* of Posthumus and Philaster?   Are all of these "stunned" into believing?   Against honest doubt the fabric of slander could never have stood for a moment, and it is but the effect of shrewd and skilful handling (common on the Elizabethan stage) that it should not even be called in question.   And for that matter, whether there is slander or not, Elizabethan heroes seldom halt betwixt two opinions or long delay a choice.   They do not fairly debate matters like the French; indeed, they do not much heed the dictates of duty or reason, but at most bring in reason to justify their virtuous or unvirtuous desires.[1]   As has been remarked by Wetz,[2] M. Faguet, and others, they, unlike the heroes of Racine and Corneille, suffer from no conflict or contention of passions.   There may be momentary revulsions, eddies or ripples in the current, as when Desdemona in her heavenly purity appears, but the stream keeps due on—

like to the Pontic Sea,
.   .   .   .
Ne'er feels retiring ebb, but keeps due on
To the Propontic and the Hellespont.

Desdemona, Juliet, Imogen forget their love or duty to parents and country— Helena, Olivia, and Perdita forget their grief for the death of father or brother—as one and all they give away their hearts and hands.[3]   But they are not therefore unsisterly, unfilial; neither does the poet intend to intimate that they "see or hear nothing but their Apollo, and that all things else have lost their worth."[4]   In the simplicity and intensity of his method and purpose, he is not careful to avoid implications which are farthest from his mind.   To his heroines sexual love is above everything; the filial Antigone was perhaps beyond the poet's range of interest; but it is doubtful if he conceived their love as devouring and swallowing up every other affection,

---

[1] Cf. Wetz, pp. 175-6.   This is, however, a very different thing from the suggestion of a subconscious undertow of passion, to be discussed later.   The debate is not fine and complete, but in the lacunae there is no intimation of incalculable forces underneath the surface.

[2] Pp. 200 f; 425-6.

[3] Olivia forgets her sorrow for her brother as soon as she sees Viola, disguised as a page. Professor Matthews (*Shakespeare,* p. 340) remarks upon Perdita's readiness "to desert her supposed father in callous unconcern at the moment when his life is threatened," but seems to explain it as I do here.   Helena "thinks not on her father" and "has forgot him" (*All's Well,* I, i, 90-4) but this may be only extravagance of expression.   Compare Rümelin on the effects of exaggeration in Shakespeare, as in implications which he did not intend.

[4] Bulthaupt, pp. 228-9.—But rightly he rejects the subtle and fantastic notion that Desdemona shows her affection sufficiently by refusing to vex her father with her presence.   That is not enough when parting from a heart-broken father, perhaps for ever.   And rightly he rejects the notion that, Cordelia-like, Desdemona has no word of comfort because she has no consciousness of wrong-doing, or, in the circumstances, thinks "to love and be silent" is kinder.

to the point of making them indifferent or harsh. And Hamlet and Brutus, the only characters who can be said to have problems, hardly present them, and soon dispose of them, without scene on scene of Cornelian debate. Only the passion is presented, not the dilemma, least of all, the ebb and flow of passion, speech by speech and scene by scene, from doubt to confidence, from resolution to indifference, from devotion to country to devotion to one's friend. A new thought, a new passion, drives out the one before; and seeing that this is still more the case in the poet's earlier period than in his prime, it must be a matter merely of the poet's art, not of psychology, still less, of an attempt at historical reconstruction.[1] If, therefore, Othello, unlike Orosmane, never again believes in his wife, it is no more that he is unable to bring his intellect to bear on the question than that he is jealous or suspicious by bent and bias.

What Mr. Rose observes concerning Othello's taking Desdemona's guilt for granted, is true, moreover, not only at the moment when he is "stunned" but throughout his course. In the temptation scene he says:

> I think my wife be honest and think she is not;
> I think that thou art just and think thou art not;

but by that the poet expresses only the conventional uncertainty of jealousy.[2] It is an emotional matter and no more. He calls not a single statement of Iago's in question, before or afterward. "You would be satisfied?" asks Iago. "Would? Nay, I will." "Death and damnation!" is his answer to Iago's reply, and forthwith he "snatches" at the "exsufflicate and blown surmises" of Iago's proofs—the dream and the handkerchief. *C'est certain, répondit Panther; il ne reste plus qu'à le prouver!* The oath follows hard upon. And even before all this he is continually taking her guilt for granted, though as yet he has had no proof at all.

> What sense had I of her stolen hours of lust?

he cries as he reappears after Iago has pocketed the handkerchief. Before that, as we have seen, he feels the pain in his forehead even in his lady's beatific presence. And, still earlier, he asks, "Why did I marry?" thinks it

---

[1] See Wetz (48-50, 86-88, 251-3), who thinks the abruptness of his art, as in *Henry VI*, is only his way of painting impulsive, semi-barbarous times, and calls in anthropology and Benvenuto Cellini to bear him out, though he himself recognizes that in a later play of an earlier time, as *Richard II*, the barons do not change their allegiance so frivolously. Titus Andronicus has two thoughts—but one at a time—to honor his dead sons and to honor Saturninus. To honor his sons he kills Tamora's son, and yet expects her to be grateful to him for bringing her prisoner to Rome, where she has married an emperor. To honor Saturninus he tries to recover his daughter and kills a son who thwarts him in it. Yet after he has got from Saturninus insults for his pains, and sees his sons dragged off to execution, and Lavinia mutilated, he trusts Aaron, Saturninus, and Tamora, to the point of cutting off his hand. All this Wetz thinks much to the poet's credit, and takes for the presentation of *Menschen von einer bestimmten Entwicklung* (p. 87). Friesen and Bulthaupt demur, and who would not be aghast at such Kulturgeschichte, as of a Browning, imported into the most primitive and atrocious tragedy the hand of genius ever penned?

[2] See above, p. 12.

the curse of marriage that we can call these delicate creatures ours and not their appetites, and in the "forked plague" finds "destiny unshunnable." Only twice, and that near the beginning, does he make any head against the tide of his passion, as in the beautiful lines:

> Nor from mine own weak merits will I draw
> The smallest fear or doubt of her revolt,
> For she had eyes and chose me;

and again:

> I do not think but Desdemona's honest:

but, immediately, on he is swept again by the Propontic current—

> And yet how Nature erring from itself . . .

"Stunned" or not, Othello is Iago's—never more Desdemona's—from the moment when first the Ancient "echoes" his words. *Dès le premier mot, tout est dit, tout est décidé. Adieu pour jamais Desdemona, adieu Othello!* And De Broglie goes on aptly to say that we follow their course not with the restless curiosity which turns again and again from fear to hope, but with something of the inexpressible anguish which takes possession of us when at a court of justice we see the futile struggles of wretches dragged to an indubitable condemnation.[1]

All the rest of what Mr. Rose has to say finds as little support in the text. Where is the slightest trace of "fluttering"? Othello uses no judgment, indeed, but, whether in conversation or in soliloquy, there is not a hitch in his mental processes or a sign of constraint. Mr. Rose's argument amounts almost to this: Othello is stunned and cannot think consecutively, but, making an effort, he everywhere thinks as consecutively as any one can. As I have elsewhere shown, when a character is really making an effort, and speaking as naturally he would not speak, Shakespeare is always at pains to make the matter clear.[2]

Giles[3] has a bit of psychology very similar to this of Mr. Rose. On Othello's farewell to his profession "Farewell the plumèd troop," etc., he remarks: "Othello does not here allude to his present grief or to his recent happiness; but, with a terrible spring of the mind, he leaps the chasm of affliction into which he cannot dare to look, and alights on the other side, amidst the turmoils of his youth, amidst the noise and glories of his soldiership. This is the instinct of the mind to save itself from madness," etc. The critic seems not to appreciate the simple purport of apostrophe in Elizabethan dramatic technique, which had not yet eliminated lyrical and de-

---

[1] Furness, p. 452.

[2] That is, by aside or soliloquy, or by the context. Cf. my articles, "Anachronism," pp. 561-2, 568; "Falstaff," p. 233. Compare, in the *Maid's Tragedy*, III, i, the mirth of Amintor, the forced character of which is made perfectly apparent.

[3] Furness, p. 201-2.

clamatory elements. And he is evidently following in the steps of Coleridge
when he finds in Hamlet's digression on wassailing "a desire to escape from
the impending thought," and his tendency (as Coleridge conceives it) "to run
off from the particular to the universal, in his repugnance to personal and
individual concerns."[1] In the steps of both follows Mr. Frank Harris[2]
when he remarks on Romeo's and Hamlet's peculiar habit of talking to themselves, ever ready to unpack their hearts with words, and on Hotspur's
loquacity, despite the fact that he has not "the gift of tongue" and "professes
not talking." Which is as much as to ignore the fact that from beginning
to end the Elizabethan dramatic method was founded on speech and outcry,
that scenes such as that in *Justice* where with never a syllable the prisoner
paces his cell and pounds on the door, or such as that in *The Second Mrs.
Tanqueray,* where Paula's secret is gathered by Ellean merely from the expression of her face, were things as yet undreamed. In Shakespeare "the
secret'st man of blood," like Richard, Macbeth, or Iago, must be vouchsafed
soliloquies and even some few confidences to others,[3] as well as a lover like
Romeo, a dreamer like Hamlet, and a boon-companion like Falstaff; and on
his stage William the Silent could no more have been suffered to hold his
tongue than is Master Silence of Gloucestershire.[4]

Instead of being stunned Othello is, we have seen, excited. The only
cases of such momentary paralysis in Shakespeare are those which Mr.
Rose has noticed: Desdemona after Othello's visit to her as a courtesan,[5]
and Macduff when he hears of his wife and children's death. Similarity
there is none. Othello does not, like them, repeat the words he hears in a
blank, unmeaning way, and his thoughts neither halt nor wander. On the
contrary he is at once aroused, "frighted," as he confesses, and all intent
upon Iago's every syllable and gesture. His passion flames steadily higher
and higher, moreover, and it is upon the depiction of this that the dramatist's
art is expended, not upon the devious mental processes from which it might
arise or by which it might be accompanied. His mind works straightfor-
wardly, so far as it can be said independently to work at all. When Iago
leaves him he thinks for himself, in his soliloquy,[6] of his lacking the soft

---

[1] *Lectures on Shakespeare* (Bohn ed., 1900, p. 355). Coleridge then proceeds to take notice
of a far more relevant consideration—the fact that "by entangling the attention of the audience
[and of the characters on the boards, we may add] Shakespeare takes them completely by surprise on
the appearance of the Ghost." And he might have gone farther, and have observed, that besides
being dramatically effective, these casual and incidental remarks of Hamlet's are, if not psychologically significant, at least very natural and human. See below, p. 66, note.

[2] Pp. 11-12, 89-90.

[3] See above, p. 27, note.

[4] See Dr. M. L. Arnold's *Soliloquy in Shakespeare* for evidence that many short soliloquies
are given to characters simply to occupy them till others arrive to talk to. The familiar business
of yawning, lighting lamps, undressing, or the like, was apparently not in use.

[5] IV, ii, 96-102.

[6] III, iii, 258 ff.

parts of conversation and his being descended into the vale of years,—matters which Iago had not urged. That of itself shows that he is not stunned, and is neither forcing his mind nor helplessly fluttering as he goes from one minor point to another.

The implication of any theory of stunning or blinding is really equivalent to the notion that Othello is dull and stupid, and, indeed, it is far truer to Shakespeare to betake ourselves to that opinion without ado. A mind which is so easily incapacitated is as good as no mind, and if that Shakespeare had meant, he would certainly at once have made his meaning clear. He was the last man to take the longest way about. And the same may be said to all the other psychological theories. "On matters like that Othello cannot think," says Sir Walter Raleigh, who may be thought to speak for the best orthodox opinion; "he is accustomed to impulse, instinct, and action; these tedious processes of arguing on dishonor are torture to him; and when he tries to think, he thinks wrong."[1] He thinks well enough, of course, until Iago takes him in hand; and it is hard to see how a man such as is here described could have been a general at all.

"He has arrived at full middle age," says Mr. Brooke admirably, "and has won the trust and respect of the most jealous and difficult of governments. All men honour his integrity, his skill in war, his ability in governing men, his self-governance, his temperate nature, a ruler of men who rules himself. He has also seen the world and mixed with many men and events in an adventurous youth: . . . a man, then, not liable to give his trust·rashly, to act on mere suspicion, without inquiry, to be ignorant of the evil which is in men. Yet this is the great improbability which Shakespeare creates for him—"[2]

though by turning it into a blind, deaf, unreasonable Chance Mr. Brooke, to be sure, surmounts it. The fact is, Othello thinks wrong not merely when dishonor is touched upon but at every turn of Iago's transparent and unplausible imposture.

It is all very well to repeat that Othello is naïve, simple, unanalytical, accustomed only to impulse and action; but a child or a savage, we in turn must repeat, has common sense. No one short of an idiot or a "criminal born" would think Iago's lies about the dream and the stolen handkerchief cause for falling straightway to one's knees and swearing to kill one's wife. Without inquiry, without weighing the evidence or the motives of the slanderer, without leaving the stage or even drawing back a bit from the brink of the terrible moment—surely, if we put convention aside, either the Moor was jealously eager for her death, or, if any one ever did, he allowed "that capability and godlike reason to fust in him unused."[3]

---

[1] 141-2. Cf. Bradley, p. 189.

[2] *Op. cit.*, pp. 173-4.

[3] Wetz, pp. 378-80, in attempting to refute Bulthaupt when he declares that if Othello and the other characters had had a grain of Iago's wit he could never have had his way, dwells upon the

It is quite impossible, however, that Shakespeare should have had it in mind to present a fool or a dolt. Wetz himself says that Iago's method— of inflammation rather than argument and proof—is always the method in Shakespeare, though his heroes are meant not only to have the normal amount of intelligence on which Bulthaupt insists[1] but even to be clever. Only in these sympathetic, degenerate days—and then less often on the stage than in the more expensive playbooks—shall you find heroes with weak faces and a weaker wit. It is contrary to the Shakespearean and Elizabethan spirit generally that in tragedy a hero should be less than his name. A villain, now and then, he may be, but never a dupe or gull. And whenever Shakespeare does intend to represent stupidity it is as evident as when he intends to represent a villain or a coxcomb. Besides, all the other characters, more especially Desdemona and Emilia (and there are not wanting those who say it) must, then, labor under the same imputation, and be stupid too.[2] Where everybody is stupid nobody is stupid, just as where everybody is "wilful, headstrong, forthputting and intolerant of opposition," as in *Romeo and Juliet* he is by Professor Matthews[3] taken to be, we had better at once put aside our doctrines of heredity and family likeness, and look to the author's technique, the artistic cipher or shorthand of his intention.

This stupidity is purely a matter of implication, being inferred from the improbability of the intrigue and the grossness of the imposition, just as wilfulness and regardlessness of consequences are inferred from a violent and unmotived plot. In general it may be laid down that not so in Shakespeare (or perhaps in any playwright) is stupidity depicted—that is, indirectly, by intentional (still less, unintentional) improbabilities and inconsequences in the action—but by the words in its mouth. Incoherence in structure does not mean stupidity in the character any more than, as we have seen, it means fate, chance, or luck, in the world. Roderigo is a case in question,

---

fact that the most intelligent people may be blinded by passion. He does not consider that that is beside the question, which is whether Shakespeare represents Othello's obtuseness as due to passion (he is blind enough, we have seen, before his passion is aroused), and also, if he does, how in the world Desdemona and the rest get blinded too.

[1] Wetz, p. 378.

[2] It is true that nowadays—and possibly it was the case in Shakespeare's time as well— Othello's endless repetition of "honest" at moments when he is being "led by the nose as tenderly as asses are" has been known to make the pit titter or laugh outright. Bulthaupt says he has observed this, and I have done so myself. But this can be considered only a miscalculation of effects, not unheard of among dramatists to-day. Cf. Brandes, p. 443, and below, p. 41, note.

[3] I do not wish to suggest that Romeo is not rash and impetuous, for in his defiance of fate before and after Juliet's death, as well as in the Friar's reproofs, it sufficiently appears. But I cannot see that the poet means to present the trait of wilfulness in Juliet, the Friar, and the Prince. Tybalt of course is a fire-eater, but Capulet is violent, as Wetz says, only as all the other Shakespearean fathers are when they are crossed—one might add, as all masculine Shakespearean characters are. Rage, violence, the extremest statement, the rashest and most intemperate conduct, and ill-considered deeds of blood, are to be reckoned against villains and heroes alike; and consequently, it being so manifestly the thing on the stage to do, we can no more turn it all into character than we can the wit, the splendid poetry, the obscenity, which, now and then, is put into almost anybody's mouth.

being a ninny primarily by virtue of what he says and what Iago says about him, by virtue of what he does and not what he fails to do; and only the inflexible consistency of German criticism would have him besotted by his passion as well as the Moor. Even Roderigo is not stupid enough to have been duped and gulled as he is; having received at the outset Iago's confession of diabolical duplicity and a willingness to serve others only in order to serve himself, it is impossible that he should have been continually handing over to him money and jewels and doing his dirty work, without anything in return but impudence.[1] If it were not for the exigencies of the plot, what he says at the end of the second scene of the fourth act about being "fobbed," which makes Gervinus say (strangely enough, though, if convention be forgotten, not without reason) that he surpasses the General in acuteness,[2] even a ninny such as he would have said long before. The merest simpleton might well begin to be suspicious after being told nine times in fifty lines to "put money in his purse,"[3] and before that purse is empty.

So, if it were not for the plot, Emilia would have spoken up about the handkerchief when she saw that Desdemona was distressed about it, and that the Moor himself, as she remarks, was jealous. "In fact," says Professor Bradley in all good faith, "she never thought of it. . . . Her stupidity in the matter is gross, but it is stupidity and nothing worse." Worse by far, for it is out of character,[4] or, you might say, with character it has nothing to do. To be sure, she does not keep silent (an objection which Mr. Bradley probably has it in mind to meet) for fear of Iago[5]—her undaunted loyalty when questioned later by Othello, before and after he has killed his wife, establishes that. But it is she, not Desdemona, who divines his jealousy; it is she who, twice over,[6] suspects "some busy and insinuating rogue" as the cause of it; and why, then, should her shrewdness and her eagerness to serve her lady not prompt her to speak up about the handkerchief on the spot, or at least to demand it again of Iago, in case it transcended her imagination to conceive that he was the rogue himself?[7]

---

[1] Wetz (p. 270) makes it the blinding of passion, but Flathe, whom he quotes with disapproval, hard-headedly thinks it strange for Iago to show Roderigo that he himself is not to be trusted.

[2] P. 531.

[3] I, iii.

[4] Bulthaupt, *op. cit.,* pp. 232-33.

[5] Traumann, *Jahrbuch,* xxxi, p. 252. This is the motive once given in the novel (Furness, p. 384) for her failure to disclose his plot, but Shakespeare, had he meant the like, would have been more explicit. From silence we can infer nothing, (see my articles *Anachronism in Shakespeare Criticism.* and *Hamlet and Iago, Kittredge Anniversary Papers,* p. 271); and Emilia's sturdy fidelity, for which Shakespeare owes nothing to Cintio, puts it in this case quite out of the question.

[6] IV, ii, 15; 131 f.

[7] Shakespeare, of course, felt the weakness, and tried to lift us over the thin ice by the threefold repetition of "my husband!" at the end. It had been "unimaginable," as the critics say of Othello and Posthumus. But this is a bit of dramaturgy, not psychology or life. It is impossible that so shrewd and worldly-minded a woman should not have suspected the busy Iago

Any dramatist who, in a similar plight, should admit of the defence that the critics set up for Shakespeare would be jeered at to his dying day. In fact this "stupidity" or forgetting is only another instance of the besetting sin of criticism, the confounding of fact and fiction, of literature and life. It is like arguing the prodigiousness of Iago's powers of dissimulation and self-control from his success in imposture;[1] or Falstaff's bravery from his going into battle and jesting there;[2] or Amintor's personal charm from the fact that he has brave Melantius for a friend and two beautiful ladies to die for lack of his love.[3] From fact no doubt such inferences may rightly enough be drawn, as in reading biography or history; but in fiction the qualities in question, unless by other means they indeed achieve realization, can have no existence whatever. How could he but succeed—how could he but jest—how could he but be hopelessly loved—seeing that such is the story, seeing that *ainsi le veut l'auteur?*

The explanation of Schlegel—her "sinful levity," which prompts her "not to confess to the taking of the handkerchief"[4]—simply makes another breach in her character in order to fill up this, taking no account of the heartiness of her advocacy later, first to the Moor, then to Iago, and then to the Moor again after her lady's death. And thus her death scene, as she plays the swan and sings "willow, willow," already so alien to her stout character as to be a bit sentimental, becomes irritating in the extreme. Schlegel, to be sure, *in vieler Hinsicht kein Mann,*[5] was, for all his learning and insight, hardly the one to understand how a woman could speak lightly and loosely of the marriage tie and yet to her mistress be staunch and true; but it is not among the least of Shakespeare's glories that the like cannot be said of him.

(who had wooed her to steal the handkerchief, had snatched it, and told her to hold her tongue) now that all this trouble is brewing under her nose. The improbability lies deep—not in her character, but in the convention of the villain who can have free play only by dint of no one knowing his nature, not even his wife. Professor Matthews (p. 243), cited below, accounts it one of Shakespeare's improvements upon the *novella* that Emilia should be without suspicion—that Iago should, by inference, have been clever enough to deceive his wife as he does every other mortal. He *does* deceive her, but is *not* clever enough.

[1] Bradley, p. 217. This, indeed, is the process by which all the orthodox have arrived at the notion of his "superhuman art." (See note above). So Professor Matthews (p. 247): "He has a self-control so marvelous that he impresses all who know him as bluff and plain-spoken," etc. In life it is hard, but in a play it is easy, and I should marvel at the poet's art more if Iago's had met with difficulties, and before the last scene were by some people suspected, like Tartuffe's. "Where they do agree on the stage," cries Mr. Puff, "their unanimity is wonderful." To Puff, no doubt, the reiteration of the word "honest"—fifteen times on the lips of others, says Mr. Bradley, and some half dozen on Iago's own—would have carried conviction, though to us it makes his success the more incredible. In the end, we have seen, it makes at least an untutored audience titter. Unanimity at the poet's fiat counts for next to nothing, and in real life so importunate a reputation for simple truth-telling would be worse than no reputation at all. It is another case of Shakespeare's overdoing the matter.

[2] See my article, "Falstaff."

[3] G. C. Macaulay, *Francis Beaumont,* p. 138.

[4] Furness, p. 432.

[5] Eckermann, Gespräche (1910), p. 497, Goethe's own remark.

As for Desdemona, we have seen already that according to Professor Bradley she too does not "remember" that she had used the handkerchief for Othello's head in the scene preceding. According to others she is so "stupid" (the highbred and delicate maiden!) as to prevaricate when he asks her for it, instead of calling Emilia to witness that she had just been complaining of its loss; so stupid as not to read in him the signs of jealousy betimes, and as to turn to pestering him with the suit of the only man (this too she does not see) who could possibly put Othello to the "ill thinking" which she had just presaged; so stupid as, having read the signs before the scene is over, to fail to concern herself further about the cause of them, or about any relief she might bring either to her lord or to herself. For the matter of that, she is still harping on Cassio in Act IV, where she enlists Lodovico in his favor and by her tactlessness provokes her husband in public to strike her in the face.

Everybody else is taken in by Iago, moreover, and the play becomes the tragedy of fools. Cserwinka, at least, makes it a play of misunderstandings, a *tragedy* of errors, we might say. And Berger, the recent director of the Burgtheater in Vienna, an admirer of the poet, a constant producer of his plays, says as much of all of them. "Ever and again the subject of his plays is the way men mistake the world and thereby come to ruin, or are shown to be fools. . . But always Shakespeare conceives this illusion of passion which possesses his heroes as something totally senseless and crazy. Justifiable passion as the motive force which brings about the tragic conflict is wholly unknown to him. . . . In comedy the joke, in tragedy the serious issue, depend only on deception or delusion."[1] No doubt the writer has in mind such otherwise clever folk as Beatrice and Benedick, who, on hearsay, fall head over heels in love, and Falstaff, who in *Henry IV* is led into ridiculous plights from which only his ready wit can extricate him, and in the *Merry Wives* is duped and cheated again and again; or such otherwise clever folk as are taken in by the slandering or dissembling of Shylock, Don John, the Antonio of *Measure for Measure,* Richard, Edmund, Goneril and Regan, Iago, Iachimo, and Cymbeline's Queen, and thereby are plunged into calamity themselves or are made to plunge their dearest into it before them. Moved in a moment, as are two of these victims, by the word of an outwardly coarse and cynical, inwardly diabolical subaltern, or an avowed disbeliever in woman's virtue who has life, property, and his disreputable reputation hanging in the balance, the one to the point of stifling a guiltless young bride in her bed, the other to the point of ordering her death by a servant's hand—in these, if anywhere in a tragic conflict, rational and "justifiable passion" is far indeed to seek.

What Berger says is true, however, only if we ignore the convention—

---

[1] *Jahrbuch* xlix, p. 189.

the stage language—and the improbabilities at which Shakespeare and his generation did not stick. Really his is not a "great stage of fools," for the defects in motivation, the preposterous impositions whether of slanderous villain or of practical joker, fairy or human, are not meant uniformly to reflect character as they would today. Dramatic art had not yet heard so clear a call as it has since, to approximate to the "modesty of nature." The plot which develops austerely out of the characters, without conspiracy or deliberate contriving, whether of the characters or of the presiding poet, would have seemed, even had Elizabethans known such a plot, a tame, unexpeditious affair. It would not have permitted them to tell out the story on the stage, as was their wont and delight, from beginning to end. And it would not have provided the temptations and persuasions, the "sudden alterations" and conversions, the contrasts of character with character and contradictions within the character itself, which offend our taste, indeed, but, because of the theatrical interest and effect afforded, rejoiced the Elizabethans. The people themselves, as well as their poet, would have chosen that, before they became jealous, Othello and Posthumus and Philaster should be the fine and generous fellows that they are, and that they should fall suddenly, unwittingly, into a traitor's snare. And they too would have chosen that at the end these heroes should emerge again, in their greatness undiminished. By the *sibi constet* they were never cheated out of their pleasure at a play. Not that, as some critics incline to think,[1] character was then more mobile and mercurial than now, any more than that Elizabethan wickedness was more villainous. Nothing could be more unscientific than to charge the romantic inequalities of Elizabethan art directly to the account of Elizabethan character and temper. Their art so far o'er-steps the modesty of nature, not because their nature, but because their notions of nature—notions of "modesty"—were less limited and refined than ours. It is only our naïve inclination to realism (the besetting sin, again, though now under cover of learning and history) which prompts us to find a picture of the times, rather than an exhibition of an irregular and "Gothic" taste, in the *miles gloriosus*, in conscious, gloomy or gloating villains,[2] in the

---

[1] See below, pp. 54-5.

[2] Against the views expressed in my article "Criminals in Shakespeare" it was urged at the Modern Language Association, a few years since, that criminals then were different, their conscious villainy and hostility to Heaven having been brought about by the Calvinism or Machiavellism of the time. What is so evidently primitive art, a self-consciousness, whether in good or in evil, to be found in drama the world over, where Calvinism or Machiavellism never raised its head, and in better drama not extinct until some score of years ago, the critic was determined to make out to be a psychological reality, just as other critics have conceived that humorous conception the Braggart Soldier to be a typical character of the Alexandrian conquest or of the Spanish domination in Italy, or the Spanish, Italian, and Elizabethan maidens roaming about unrecognized in hose and doublet to be characteristic of Renaissance high life. No doubt there was in Elizabethan conduct a vein of self-consciousness not apparent now: Sidney's, Donne's, and Herbert's exits from the scene prove that. But that was due to the fact that public opinion had not yet established a standard of taste and common sense. And I am not aware of the slightest evidence that

violent and unreasonable changes from virtue to vice or vice to virtue, in the superfluous atrocities perpetrated on the stage, or in the indecencies incidentally uttered or relished by pure-minded ladies like Helena or Desdemona.[1] In the last some scholars who read the unprintable anecdotes of the time, think to find no offence to art, seeing that then the like were uttered and relished by the finest ladies without offense to decency. Which is as much as to say that Shakespeare could not reach beyond the facts, that his taste was not fallible but his imagination feeble, and that his genius was by no means what it has always been taken to be! What Shakespeare's intention is (however he may neglect it) plainly appears from Desdemona's later confession:

> I cannot say 'whore :'
> It doth abhor me now to speak the word.

And her pleasure in the Ancient's smutty jests is not in character at all.

As for the remaining theory, that the circumstances of Othello and Desdemona's union were dubious, and "that a love thus grounded in disparity is always unstable," it is to be found in conjunction either with the orthodox theory,[2] or with the theory of Schlegel (or the various modifications of it) that Othello is the half-civilized, harem-keeping barbarian, or, merely because of the extraordinary circumstances and Brabantio's warning,[3] is suspicious or anxious from the first.[4] In the one case these circumstances can, consistently, be made to affect him only through Iago's suggestion; in the other they are the ground and basis of the barbarian's fears. As before, the orthodox interpretation is less foreign to the text. Often it has been asserted that the union seems extraordinary or unnatural to everybody.[5]

---

then men were at all more conscious of the abysses of their own depravity or of the heights of their rectitude. If in the former case they were, how did they manage to exist? "A certain approval of conscience," says Carlyle, "is essential even to physical existence." But, as in the above article, I rest my case, not on psychology and surmises concerning the history of civilization, but on evidence drawn from the history of dramatic art. The character's consciousness of his utter villainy is only one of many points at which drama took as yet the absolute rather than the relative point of view, and thus showed that it was incompletely differentiated from the lyric and the epic. There is complacence in the speech of the good, grandiloquence in the speech of the great, and every emotion is inclined to be self-conscious. Anybody may discuss himself in soliloquy, acknowledge his own virtue or wickedness, nurse and measure his joy or sorrow, or forget the cause of his emotion in his external attitude to the emotion itself. The very language is rhetorical and declamatory, descriptive, external. Even in the matter of stage-setting artists could not take the relative point of view, and as late as in D'Avenant's time a distant prospect of the City of Rhodes furnished the decoration for scenes which were laid within the city walls.

[1] In Helena's ribald conversation with Parolles (I, i), and Desdemona's lending an ear to Iago's obscene jests on the quay (*II*, i). The scholar whom I have in mind is a friend who has not yet expressed the view in print.

[2] See Bradley, p. 193; Schelling, i, p. 575.

[3] Gervinus lays stress upon this, and once comes near to interpreting it as an effective curse in the style of *Schicksalstragödie* and *Richard III*. Cf. pp. 520, 521, 529.

[4] Wetz, p. 287 f.

[5] Wolff, ii, 170-171; Brooke, pp. 171-2; 190-1. Contrast what Professor Brandl has to say, p. 162, on the attitude of the other characters . . . Even Brabantio, he observes, has been wrought

Really the only one shocked by it is Brabantio : Iago dares to cast aspersions upon it only in his presence, Othello's, and Roderigo's. After the Moor has killed his wife, Emilia tells him that she was too fond of her most filthy bargain, but the woman had said nothing of the sort before. And, like every one else, the Duke and Senate at the beginning and Lodovico and Gratiano at the end show the Moor only respect and admiration, and treat the marriage itself as above reproach. The Duke declares, when Othello's great speech is ended, that he thinks

> this tale would win my daughter too;

and, again, as he concludes the deliberations,

> If virtue no delighted beauty lack,
> Your son-in-law is far more fair than black.

When Lodovico sees Othello strike his wife he has nothing to say against marrying Moors or strangers, either with or without a parent's leave, but is simply amazed that this can be

> the noble Moor whom our full Senate
> Call all in all sufficient,

thinks his wits must not be safe, and is "sorry."

The whole situation is presented as in no way "unnatural," whether in itself or in the eyes of the world; and Othello neither has aspirations to ally himself with the higher race nor suffers through racial intolerance or prejudice.[1] He is happy to marry Desdemona, but not because she is a white woman or the daughter of a magnifico. And he speaks of his blackness as the cause of Desdemona's unfaithfulness but once—because Iago had urged it—and turns immediately to other causes—his unpolished manners and his age :—

> Haply for I am black[2]
> And have not those soft parts of conversation
> That chamberers have, or for I am declined
> Into the vale of years.

upon by the enemies of Othello. Wolff says that in the eyes of the world the marriage is a *Missehe* and is unnatural. Brandl is right in affirming the contrary. Wetz (p. 292), to the same effect; and he aptly remarks upon the fact that Montano (II, i, 60-5) does not wonder at Othello, negro though he be, being able to marry a Venetian lady who "paragons description and wild fame."

[1] This is Schröer's view, as if *Othello* or the *Merchant of Venice* were Ibsenian social drama. *Titus Andronicus*, pp. 122-3: "Das Opfer seiner tragischen, zitternden Hoffnung, dass ihm, dem Angehörigen der fremden Rasse, doch die Liebe eines edlen Christenmädchens zu Theil werden könne. Othello fällt durch die Intoleranz oder durch seine durch fremde Intoleranz bis zum sträflichen Misstrauen und Unglauben gesteigerte Empfindlichkeit." The "Intoleranz" Shakespeare's art was equal to presenting, but there is no evidence that he attempted the task.

[2] Black he certainly is, and a negro, as some of the best recent critics, such as Dr. Furness and Dr. Bradley, have made clear. It is all well enough to remind us that in Shakespeare and other Elizabethans black often means "of a dark complexion," but of course Desdemona would not be quitting him for Cassio because of that. And Furness's proof drawn from Othello's

As we have seen, he is not of himself anxious or suspicious: the disparity of the union has, for the moment at least, only made him beautifully humble and grateful—

> For she had eyes and chose me—

and neither does he reproach himself with an ill-assorted union nor, before or after his jealousy, does he or Desdemona or any one else show that consciousness of a lack of sympathy, due to short acquaintance[1] or inequality of age, which the critics insist upon, or due to racial differences in manners and customs, or to the misunderstandings arising from differences in physiognomic expression, which Mr. Bradley detects.[2] The truly Elizabethan character of the play appears from the fact that all the differences in rank, age, race and color, physiognomic expression, and point of view, which in a modern play or novel would act directly upon man and wife to alienate them, here have effect only as urged by the malignant lips of Iago, and that of these only the obvious, palpable ones are urged—race, color, rank, and age.[3]

More than on these, however, Iago insists upon the sensual, deceitful propensities of the fair Venetians, and Othello responds to the suggestion as to every other that Iago makes. If at this point we are to grant what Mr. Bradley himself would refuse to grant (but Wetz and the others assume) that the suspiciousness and jealousy are lurking or slumbering already in his heart—then this consciousness of the newly married man, who has not

words is unanswerable: "Her name that was as fresh as Dian's visage, is now *begrim'd and black* as mine own face." Cf. also Eckhardt, *op. cit.*, p. 174. A striking proof that the word *Moor* was, as among the Germans at this time, exactly equivalent to *negro*, is not only its use as applied to the curly-haired, thick-lipped Aaron in *Titus Andronicus*, but also the constant interchange of the two words as applied to the equally unmistakable negro Eleazar, in *Lust's Dominion* (pub. 1657). Cf. Hazlitt's Dodsley xiv, pp. 135, 158; and Eckhardt, p. 175, as to Brome's *English Moor*.

[1] This is a circumstance insisted upon by many of the Germans, by Dowden (p 207), and by Bradley (p. 192).

[2] P. 193. See my article *Anachronism in Shakespeare Criticism*, pp. 561-2. Mr. Bradley condemns Schlegel's notion of Othello as a half-civilized barbarian because it imports modern Kulturgeschichte into the text, but he proceeds to import a still subtler racial psychology of his own. As Wolff says (ii, p. 167), "Nichts ist falscher als besondere Merkmale der schwarzen Rasse an Othello zu suchen," (p. 168), "keine volkspsychologische Studie." Or, as Mr. Bradley himself says, at p. 210: "With him (Shakespeare) the differences of period, race, nationality, and locality have little bearing on the inward character . . . . When he does lay stress on such differences his intention is at once obvious." And yet this notion of race psychology is continually reappearing, even in those who, like Mr. Bradley, turn their backs on Schlegel—in Gervinus, Ulrici, Bulthaupt (*op. cit.*, pp. 233-4), and Eckhardt, p. 174 (Ein echter Neger . . in seiner geradezu kindlichen Vertrauensseligkeit . . . wohl auch in der kühnen Todesverachtung, mit der er sich am Schluss selbst ersticht); but it is the palefaced Posthumus and Philaster, and not another Moor, who also exhibit these traits, though their hands are stayed. The Zeitgeist is of all spirits the most difficult to exorcise. But really the notion first appears not in Schlegel at all, but, like many another vagary of Shakespeare criticism, in Maurice Morgann, in 1777, *Falstaff* (1820), p. 64.

[3] Iago does not speak of age to Othello at all, but repeatedly to himself and Roderigo. Othello himself, however, speaks, in his soliloquy, of it and of his lack of polished manners, as if both things, one might suppose, had been suggested by Iago. See above, p. 45. It may be that the poet had a lapse of memory.

yet "lived with his wife for months and years," that "he is under the spell of a feeling which can give glory to the truth but can also give it to a dream,"[1] is simply a finer name for the "uneasiness" and uncertainty of the Germans.[2] Like the racial differences in physiognomic expression, moreover, it suffers from the further disability of not finding any vestige of representation in the text; and if Shakespeare's conception and intention are to be ignored, we had better make a clean sweep of the matter and turn out an Othello as predisposed and psychological—as German—as we can. Not once does the poet suggest that Othello "could not have known much of Desdemona;" on the contrary

> her father loved me; oft invited me;
> Still questioned me the story of my life.

He told it all, and to Desdemona once told it over again; Cassio "went between us very oft;" and Othello courted her by word—

> upon this hint I spake—

as well as by letter.

All this, however, is neither here nor there: in Shakespeare and the Elizabethan drama acquaintance or lack of acquaintance counts for little, whether in matters of love or of confidence.

> Who ever loved that loved not at first sight,

like Marlowe's Hero and Leander, like Shakespeare's Rosalind and Orlando, Romeo and Juliet, Olivia and Viola, Miranda and Ferdinand? And are these youths and maidens destined to matrimonial shipwreck, every one?[3] The noble Leonato, moreover, is as ready to think his daughter foul as if he did not know her;[4] Lear knows not Goneril, Regan, or Cordelia, but judges them simply by the words that they speak; Gloster trusts Edmund, who has been "out nine years," rather than the noble Edgar—and Edgar must needs trust him too[5]—who has stayed under his eye at home; and Posthumus

---

[1] Bradley, pp. 192-3. Somewhat the same idea is expressed by Mr. Brooke, pp. 190-1.

[2] Wolff, ii, p. 170, so far as the lack of acquaintance is concerned.

[3] Troilus and Cressida love "right for the firste sighte" (1. 669), and on that basis one might quite as properly explain Cressida's infidelity, though it is far from Chaucer's thought. (For I cannot but consider Professors Cook and Root's interpretation of the character as artful and faithless from the beginning to be a symptom of that same modern craving for unity which has thwarted the intention of the author in the characters of Falstaff, Hamlet, and Othello). One has to remember that these earlier poets were not careful to provide the "grounds of belief," and a psychological foundation for confidence or affection. Often in Renaissance drama a glimpse in passing, a picture, or even another's report of the beauty, is enough. In any case we must be measurably consistent, and it is very strange that critics like Professor Bradley should attribute Othello's lack of confidence in Desdemona to his lack of acquaintance, and yet not stick at the improbability of his confidence in a horribly wicked man, from whom, as Mr. Brooke admits, he "must have felt a natural repulsion," and whom, so far as we know, he has not known intimately at all— though the more he knew him, to be sure, the more improbable still his confidence might be.

[4] *Much Ado*, IV, i, 116 ff.

[5] Cf. Pellissier, p. 240, who justly remarks on the unplausibleness of Edgar's taking Edmund's word for it that his father is in a fury with him, without either distrusting his brother or seeking an explanation from his father. Cf. Bradley, p. 257.

puts faith in the stranger rather than in Imogen, whom he loved, with whom he had been bred and reared.[1] And what good in the world would it do Othello to have known Desdemona longer, seeing that he puts faith in Iago, who has not been his friend, rather than in his friend and the wife of his bosom?[2] Indeed, with the Elizabethans, as with the psychologically uninitiate today, rather prevailed the romantic notion that the newly wedded and blissful husband should be less likely to lean to suspicion than "he who had lived with a wife for months and years." Iago's opinion, constantly reiterated, as to the time for that—when their passions shall have begun to pall[3]—is certainly far closer to Shakespeare's own than is the critics'. The question, however, simply did not concern the unpsychological, story-telling Elizabethan dramatic art. Quite as often, in fact, jealousy arises in lovers and the newly married as in those whose passion has run its course; yet that is due, not to the author's convictions and opinions, but rather to Elizabethan delight in the story as a whole, and in sweeping changes—love at its highest pitch flung flaming into jealousy and hate.

If for no other reason, psychology cannot be made out of the circumstance that Othello is newly married because of the vaunted system of "double time."[4] For though according to the direct and explicit references of the plot Othello is tempted the day after the wedding night and Desdemona strangled thirty-six hours after her arrival in Cyprus, according to numerous incidental remarks and the general treatment of the characters and their relations to each other it would seem that Othello and Desdemona had lived together for weeks or months. Where there is a "double clock" there is little foundation for theories of experience and reality—for psychology, in short.[5]

[1] Without his knowing it, Imogen herself, with even less excuse, had for a moment done the like. See above, p. 32, note.

[2] It is of course absurd to urge that Cassio has by his drunkenness quite forfeited Othello's esteem and respect. Even in our teetotaling days men don't think a man capable of adultery with his dearest friend's wife simply because he has given way to a momentary temptation to drink. And a few score years after Shakespeare Hobbes could find matter for boasting even in the fact that he had not been drunk above a hundred times in his life.

[3] By the device of "long time," indeed (see below, note 3), Iago is in a position to make it appear that this is on the point of coming to pass. See I, iii, 338-370; II, i, 224-252.

[4] Furness, p. 358 ff, Thorndike, *Tragedy*, pp. 163-4. The fact of the contradictory time references cannot be disputed, though for reasons which I cannot here undertake to present, I cannot accept what is now the established explanation of them. (Much nearer the truth, if not the truth itself, is Miss Buland's Yale dissertation [1912] which has just met my eye).

[5] Voltaire has been accused of doing violence to nature in *Zaïre* by crowding the full course of jealousy into the classical thirty hours, and Othello has been held up to him as a model (König, *Jahrbuch*, x, p. 269; ed. of *Zaïre* in the *Bibliothèque de la Faculté des Lettres de Lyon*, p. xxxv). By "short time," as we have seen, Shakespeare himself crowds it into thirty-six hours. But the point at issue should be, not which is superior, the classic or the romantic formula, for between the two Voltaire at least was not at liberty to choose, but which of the poets has made more of his formula, or risen farther above it. And though in many respects the two dramas are not to be mentioned in the same breath, it is doubtful whether under all the shackles of the unities Voltaire has not contrived better to convey the illusion of long time, that is, of development. At

En art rien ne compte que d'exprimé;[1] and that is still truer of the Elizabethan drama than of ours. In Shakespeare's time poets did not leave such ideas to suggestion: what is more, they saw no such need as we moderns see of going before and preparing the way for a passion. If the general who had a tale of his love to tell like that in the Council-chamber, or the "worthy gentleman" who was blest with the heart and hand of an Imogen, could, without fit evidence or a hearing given, be brought, by a single slanderer, in an hour or so, to the point of resolving to kill his wife, you might think that any man in the world could too. And before the abyss of that conclusion the critics, ignoring convention, ignoring human nature still more, do not tremble or recoil. Ulrici and Professor Bradley, indeed, contemplate it with something of a Calvinist's fearful satisfaction, as a merit of the play.

". . *Any* man situated as Othello was would have been disturbed by Iago's communications, and I add that many would have been made wildly jealous.[2] . . . Any husband would have have been troubled by them."[3]

"I should like to see the man—in Italy, in the wealthiest commercial city of the world, and at the time of the corruption of female beauty such as is described by Iago and reflected by Emilia's loose talk, as cleverly and cunningly deceived by a friend and military comrade (whom all the world considers a man of honor), and seeing the token of his love in the hands of a young amiable man, and whose doubts, moreover, are strengthened by the warm interest of his wife in her supposed lover, who would not become suspicious, and give an ear to the whisperings of the demon of jealousy! In fact the man who would not find this to be an adequate proof of infidelity, would have, in Arcadian simplicity, to consider women angels."[4]

To such a pass of moral anarchy have we come with our confusion of life and literature, our theories of a Fate incarnate in a plot, our notion that

the one place where that illusion is indispensable, where Othello changes, Shakespeare, with weeks and months at his disposal, takes no pains to secure it. As in Greek plays such as the *Agamemnon*, the chief thing is not the bare assertion of lapse of time, but artistic arrangement,—the marking of stages and gradations, the judicious use of intervals provided in the chorus, division of scenes or acts, or conversations with minor characters, to suggest lapse of time where most it is needed. But whereas Othello becomes jealous in a single scene (from which he retires, indeed, with Desdemona, just after her heavenly appearance, but in which he appears again, jealous beyond recovery, as soon as Iago, who stays on the stage, has pocketed the handkerchief), Orosmane's first suspicion of Nérestan—or thought of a suspicion—is fanned by Zaïre's repeatedly suspicious conduct, both when she is with him and when she is with others, during the intervals of her conversations with Nérestan and Fatime, and his own with Corasmin, until, suspicious circumstances piling one upon another, he in the end resolves upon her death. See above, p. 8. In tracing this development Voltaire might have been more skilful and consistent, but develop the passion he did, and gave, at the critical moment, the impression of long time, in the face of obstacles such as Shakespeare had not to meet.

[1] Gaultier, *Le Sens de l'Art*, p. 63: the same notion is constantly implied or expressed in Lipps' *Streit der Tragödie*, as p. 27-8, though it is little remembered in criticism.

[2] So recent and scientific a critic as Eckhardt (*Dialekt- und Ausländer-typen*, p. 174) echoes this opinion.

[3] Bradley, pp. 192-4. I have reversed the order of the sentences, but the italics are the author's. Mr. Brooke, pp. 190-1, seems for the moment to be of the same opinion.

[4] Ulrici, *Shakespeare's Dramatic Art*, i, p. 408.

"in Great Drama, in the *Agamemnon*, in *Othello*, in *Hamlet*, in *Macbeth*, there is an imagination at work whose laws are inexorable, are inevitable, as the laws by the operation of which the planets move around the sun!"[1] I cannot but be reminded of Charles Lamb's protest against *George Barnwell* as holiday edification for London 'prentices: "It is really making uncle-murder too trivial to exhibit it as done upon such slight motives; it is attributing too much to such characters as Millwood. . . . Uncles that think anything of their lives should fairly petition the Chamberlain against it." So married women, if criticism is to persist in its grim and truculent course, should petition against *Othello*, for certainly it is attributing still more to such characters as Iago, whose wiles cannot, in the nature of the case, turn to account the seductions of sex.

We have narrowly examined not only Iago's preposterous proofs, which these two scholars find to be cogent, but also the previous process, the tempering of Othello, before the Ancient seals with him, like wax betwixt finger and thumb. Even from his own point of view neither Mr. Bradley nor Ulrici can be said to have done this. Mr. Bradley, to be sure, takes pains to observe that in the first stage of the temptation Othello is confused and deeply troubled, feels even horror, but is not yet jealous in the proper sense of that word.[2] But with that we need not quarrel, seeing that he admits that the passion named raises its head in the subsequent soliloquy, and has already laid hold of Othello when in the same scene he reappears. Even on Mr. Bradley's showing the man has been made jealous at a blow. And yet these two eminent scholars from whom we have quoted, together with the others of the great company of the orthodox, from Coleridge down, will have it that the like could have happened to any man! This would be hard enough to understand even if in defiance of Shakespeare's intention they held that Othello was already anxious because of the situation and was suspicious at the core; but it is all the harder when the change comes about by the "charm of woven paces and of waving hands," the ramparts of personality—love, faith, common sense, and an instinctive knowledge of the good and the wicked—needing not to be stormed or scaled. But that so they will have it is in keeping with their philosophical (rather than historical) method, their indifference to the history of the drama and to the greater approximation of dramatic art in modern times to the realities of human life and character, and their resolute intention to discover a reflection of the world as it is or as we see it, in what, devised and fitted primarily for a highly conventional stage, was not, in our modern sense, even a reflection of the world as Shakespeare saw it himself.

He was, when all is said, a dramatist, and the rift which we have found

---

[1] Article *Poetry*, by Mr. Watts-Dunton, in the *Britannica*, 11th ed., p. 885.
[2] P. 194.

in Othello's character should not too much amaze us. Dramatists as famous
as Euripides, Beaumont and Fletcher, Webster,[1] Corneille, and Molière, and
as recent as Mr. Masefield, have left the like in the creatures of their pens,
and Shakespeare and his fellows did so, as we have seen, particularly in
cases of jealousy, without stint or scruple. "Iphigenia in Aulis on her knees
in no way resembles her later self," says Aristotle[2] of one of the most moving
of Euripides' dramas; and it is not merely the heroism of her later self for
which we are not prepared, but the adult and enfranchised intelligence supplanting girlish naïveté. Evadne in Beaumont and Fletcher's *Maid's Tragedy,* thought to be "about as living a piece of human flesh as ever was put on
paper,"[3] lives in the thrilling scene in her bedchamber, in the scene with her
husband and the king, and in many a speech after it; but in her conversion,
her murder of her paramour in the capacity of a repentant and "abusèd
lady," her love for the weak Amintor, or her death, she is hardly for a
moment the proud and scornful woman "who loves her life well" and her
pleasure.[4] Corneille's tyrants and stepmothers, says Sainte-Beuve, are
wicked through and through; but at the sight of a fine action they some-

---

[1] Cf. my *John Webster,* pp. 124-7, on the character of Bosola. The rôles of tool-villain and
professional torturer, on the one hand, and of poetic meditator and indignant moralist, on the other,
are, as I show, incompatible. In the latter capacity he broods and subtilizes, calls the soul in the
body a lark in a cage, and weeps and mourns over the corpses of the Duchess and her children:
and in the former he goes roundly to his work of torture and slaughter, with no more qualms
or scruples than a Sultan's mute. When "on duty," indeed, he seems to enjoy it, and he lacerates
the Duchess' spirit far more than his devoir as a feed "executioner" requires. And I show, as now
I try to do in Othello, that the unity of the character lies in the tone and manner rather than in any
psychology, and, in this particular case, in the tone of the character's utterances when "off duty"
—when himself. It is these, and these only, that warrant Symonds' esthetic appreciation. In that
discussion I now detect a bit of overstatement, as I say that Flamineo and Bosola are not men
but malcontents and tool villains, "just as they might have been prologues and epilogues;" but
what I had in mind was the lack of unity in their characters, the incompatibility of the two
functions named, and on that I insist as much as ever. It is the same dissonance that I have
noted earlier in my book (pp. 103, 108-11) in the characters of Marston's Malevole and Tourneur's
Vendice, Flamineo's and Bosola's prototypes, who, when in disguise, play their parts in all their
hideous indecency, for all that these are worth, despite their high-mindedness when out of it.
Mr. W. W. Greg (*Modern Language Review,* October, 1906, p. 73), may call this comparative and
analytic method "absurdly superficial" if he pleases, but I am content that scholars should judge of
it, and judge between him and me.

[2] *Poetics,* xv, 5.

[3] Thorndike's *Influence of Beaumont and Fletcher,* p. 120.

[4] Cf. Mr. P. E. More, *Nation,* (N. Y.), April 24, 1913, p. 410. I cannot see how Professor
Gayley (*Beaumont,* 1914, p. 354-7) can undertake to deny that Evadne is "an incomprehensible
tangle of passions." In the scene in the bedchamber itself you do not know what to make of her.
Every speech is for situation and sensation, at almost any cost. Why should she be angry with
Amintor, whom she has cozened and whom she presently declares that she pities? Why should
she then ask him to kill the man who has wronged her, seeing that, until she is converted, she
evidently prefers him to Amintor himself? She forgets the wish as soon as it is uttered; and it
was uttered to heighten the mystery—to lead up to the promise to kiss the sin from his lips
(which adds to the shock of the oath she in a moment repeats to forbear his bed) as well as
to lead up to the disclosure of the lover's name. It prepares, too, for the still unplausible killing
of the King by her own hand. Moreover, if, as Professor Gayley thinks, she despises Amintor
for his pusillanimity, why in a moment should she confess that she lusts for him? Or, with
this feeling, why should her ruthless, shameless animal nature respect for one moment her oath
of fidelity to the King? The only answer is that to the dramatist stage-points are more precious

times face about and rally round the standard of virtue.[1] Molière's Tartuffe, subjected to the searching analysis of Lemaître,[2] turns out to be ("without the playwright's being at much pains to harmonize the two natures")[3] at first a gross hypocrite and guttler, and then, in order that he might really be the man to solicit the hand of Orgon's daughter and the favors of his wife, a clever and finished rake. It is an article of the faith that out of the characters are the issues of the plot, but Tartuffe and Othello and many another of no lesser name play the parts, and duly fill the rôles (though with a shrug, as it were), which have been destined for them.

> Tartuffe est une espèce de grossier bedeau, de rat d'église, aux façons vulgaires et basses. Pétant de santé avec cela. . . . C'est un goinfre. Il mange tout seul, à son souper, deux perdrix, avec une moitié de gigot en hachis. Il rote à table. . Un truand de sacristie, une trogne à la Callot, un pourceau béat, qui, au fond, ne doit pas être bien dangereux, qui ne demande qu'à manger, boire et dormir son soûl entre ses prières, et dont le fait est plutôt mômerie machinale et grimaces d'habitude qu'hypocrisie profonde et perverse. . . . Le second Tartuffe, élégant et redoutable, l'aventurier subtil, le fourbe renommé.[4] . . .

And Mr. Masefield's Nan, patient and plaintive under the abuse and reproaches of her aunt, once wishes that this cause of all her woes may never feel the like herself, and that Dick, who has abandoned her, may be happy with her rival; but she draws a knife upon her aunt, poisons her rival, and stabs Dick. All her meekness and unselfishness, her self-forgetful love for her lover, old Gaffer, the flowers of the field and whatsoever things are lovely in the world, belong to one woman, and her readiness with the knife to quite another.

Why should Mr. Masefield have instead of one Nan two? Because the sentiments of a true-love who makes use of knife and poison are thought to be not more acceptable than those of a husband who strikes and throttles. And yet like Shakespeare he tries with might and main to make out of his

---

than psychology, or (rather) than truth to nature. No other view can fairly be taken of her conversion at the point of the sword, though it has even been applauded as the only way of dealing with a character like hers. "There is no way but the way of violence and terror," says the excellent scholar Macaulay (*Beaumont*, p. 143); "she may be terrified into a repentance which will be none the less sincere on that account." Thus Fletcher (for the scene is his) can procure not only a confession but repentance, and Mr. Macaulay and Mr. Gayley (p. 357), can put faith in the genuineness of both. Our critics share for the moment the moral and psychological views of the Inquisition, or of Salem in the witchcraft days. At bottom it is but an old stage trick, used in the *Spanish Tragedy*, II, i, as in *Cymbeline*, III, v, 84-103, and Dolce's *Marianna;* but in these cases, as applied to underlings, to procure information alone, it has far more psychological propriety than when used to coerce the spirit of a king's paramour, who has it in her to kill both the King and herself. Truth and not a lie, a change of heart and not a bit of hypocritical imposture, are here forthcoming only because for the purposes of his play the dramatist must have it so. The psychology is like that in the *Taming of the Shrew*—sweetness elicited from a bitter spirit by bullying and abuse. And that is in a farce, a fabliau!

[1] *Portraits littéraires,* i, pp. 46.7.

[2] *Impressions de Théâtre* (1892), iv. p. 37 ff.

[3] P. 40.

[4] It is true that the grosser nature appears mainly (though not wholly) through others' report, but Molière makes it clear that this report is his own verdict and the truth.

two characters with one name but one. Nan once draws the knife on her aunt when she discovers that she has thrown her coat into the pig-wash, only that we may be prepared for her drawing it later with deadlier effect. So Othello, though in the first act he could not be ruffled, is, just before the temptation begins, allowed to get angry with Cassio, accepts Iago's report of the incident without investigation as he does more momentously later, puts off some measure of his magnificent calm, is, in a way, "tenderly led by the nose" already.[1] So, too, he is given his foreboding on the quay, and on the very brink of calamity is given (though but as if in a dream or a picture) a fleeting glimpse of it:

> Perdition catch my soul,
> But I do love thee! and when I love thee not
> Chaos is come again![2]

And to the same purpose Nan, when she stabs her lover, is made to fall into Othello's cant. "Else she'll betray more men," mutters the Moor; and Nan shrieks, "Spare those women!" as she strikes her lover to the earth. But all this smoothing and scumbling of things over, whereby the contrasts of fine acting parts and thrilling situations are made more compatible and plausible, helps the psychology not a bit. It is the "art of preparation"— the art of the theatre rather than of the analytical novel, and nowise the image of life. Nan made Jenny eat of the dead sheep and stabbed Dick neither for love of justice nor for love of her sex, just as Othello strangled his "fair devil" quite regardless of her possible future betrayal of Cassio or still "more men." Psychology (though not stage verisimilitude) demands that heroes and heroines who do jealous and vindictive deeds should have jealous and vindictive sentiments to prompt them, or, if there is a slanderer, should really be the person to lend him an ear. *Natura non facit saltum*, but Nature is by the dramatist made to appear to do so, that Art may not.

Such a change as appears in Othello appears repeatedly in Shakespeare and the Elizabethan drama, without the same pains being taken to cover it up. Fletcher and Massinger have their heroes plunge from love into jealousy even more abruptly and more unreasonably, and their ladies cry, "Chastity, I renounce thee," or "Come home again, my frighted faith, my virtue," as if they were calling or chasing away a pet.[3] Shakespeare him-

---

[1] II, iii, 204f., he gets angry before he has heard both sides.

[2] The passage has been made much of in order to prove the predisposition. At most, however, it can be considered to be a bit of dramatic hedging, an effort to make the transition to jealousy as the hour of temptation draws nigh. Very likely, however, there is no self-revelation to it, but the "when" is equivalent to "if," and "is come again" to "will come again." Cf. Furness, *ad loc.*:
> For he being dead, with him is beauty slain,
> And, beauty being dead, black Chaos comes again.
> *Venus and Adonis*, 1.1020.

Cf. *Winter's Tale*, IV, iv, 486-89.

[3] For the references see my *John Webster*, p. 178.

self has Leontes, when he hears of his son's death, converted in two lines; has Posthumus lose faith in Imogen the moment he catches sight of the bracelet; has Richard woo and win the woman who hates him, and whose husband and father-in-law he had murdered, in a single scene; and when he changes Timon, changes him from one all friendliness and generosity to one all bitterness and hate, with not a vestige of baffled affection left to tell the tale.[1] The abruptness of the transition—the length of the leap—ceases to amaze us, indeed, when we stop to consider the gulf that has been fixed between. We have no mind either to explain away or to complain of what the playwright delights in or deliberately chooses! In Greene's *Pandosto*[2] the jealousy of Leontes develops little by little, instead of bursting out of a sudden in the heart of a man who, apparently, had never known the passion before and is not to know it again. In Bandello's novel old Capulet has recourse to marriage only as a last resort after Juliet "falls into a sadness" for banished Romeo,[3] instead of one day bidding Paris seek his daughter's consent (though before marriage "two more summers must wither in their pride"), and, the next, making, for no reason discernible, "a desperate tender of his child's love" with a view to a wedding o' Thursday next. Hamlet, Iago, Lady Macbeth, and King Lear, all have in the sources reasons for their conduct more relevant or plausible than those furnished in the plays. And for all that it stood in Lodge's novel before him, why in the world should Oliver abuse, rob, and twice conspire against the life of, Orlando, if he is to have the brotherliest companionship with him afterward and mate with the true-hearted Celia in the end?[4] Oliver, Othello, Timon, and Posthumus, Anne and Elizabeth by their chief enemy persuaded, Edmund and Iachimo converted, Katharine tamed, and Benedick and Beatrice plunged head over heels in love in a trice—all these belong to an art which is so far from going before and preparing the way for a passion that it has passion, or another's eloquence, take the soul by storm and assault. The struggles of contraries—convulsions and conversions—rather than the throes of what is merely being born and bursting into life within, make up the stuff and substance of this art, as of that dramatic art which (though the trouble comes from a hand divine instead of a practical joker's or a villain's) is nearest akin to it,—the ancient.

Criticism has chosen, notwithstanding, to explain this away. Wetz, for

---

[1] One might add to the list cases such as Bertram's losing his aversion to matrimony and to Helena when at last she puts the ring on his finger; but often the dénouements of Shakespeare's comedies were frankly summary and external. That he was content to have them so, however, shows how unpsychological his conception was.

[2] Pellissier, pp. 10-11.

[4] *Ibid.*, pp. 17-18.

[4] Cases like this are numerous. The conversion of the heroine of Dekker's *Honest Whore* quite obliterates her former self. And compare the change in the lecherous old king in Fletcher's *Humorous Lieutenant*, as described in the article of Mr. More, *Nation*, May 1, 1913, p. 437.

instance, explains the conversion of Leontes and the success of Richard, like the shameful conduct of Claudio (not merely in repudiating Hero publicly but in jesting at Benedick's expense just after the news of her death), all on the basis of Renaissance character,—passionate, unreflective, running and leaping from one extreme to the other. But here is the besetting critical sin once more, and the difficulty lies not in the disposition of the people of the Renaissance but in the art with which they are presented—with which they were content.[1] Simpler men, says Wetz,[2] have stormy and passionate conversions; but that of Leontes is a recantation cool and complete.[3] He sees, and remedies, the whole error of his course in the twinkling of an eye, whereas, however primitive, a man must, in letting go his old beliefs, fumble and grope a bit into the new. Such a man might change by leaps and bounds, indeed, instead of step by step, but he would stumble and fall back again into his old ways—his old jealousy—and not put on the new man at once and for ever.

The same is to be said of the barons in the English historical plays, who yield or renounce their allegiance as occasion demands, and never regret their breach of fealty to their former sovereign until they are disposed to a breach of fealty to their present.[4] And Anne, who spits on Richard at the beginning of the scene, plights her troth to him at the end—as later Elizabeth bestows on him the hand of her daughter[5]—only on the strength of the old convention at the bottom of Iago's intrigue, the omnipotence of dissimulation[6] and persuasive arts, and another even older, the frailty of woman. It is an idle thing for Wetz and others to accumulate historical

---

[1] Mr. More, also, in the article in the *Nation* cited above, seems to make this error as he compares the incomprehensibility of characters like Evadne on the stage with the incomprehensibility of the men and women of the time. He is dwelling on immorality, and at that point, or in respect to many another trait. such as servility, or belief in the divine right of kings, comparison is justifiable enough. But what is incomprehensible in the stage figure is the motivation, the structure of the whole, and that is not a matter of Elizabethan human nature but of art.

So Taine (*Hist. Eng. Lit.*, bk. II, chap. ii) says of Marlowe: "All this is pretty strong, you will say; these people kill too readily, and too quickly. It is on this very account that the painting is a true one," etc. But it is a matter of Elizabethan taste rather than of character. And a bold undertaking it would be to show that Othello was jealous without a jealous disposition, because in the Renaissance men could dispense with the l"ce, and, when put into a play, needed no motivation. It was not the subject, but the dramatist and his audience (as such), that had no need of it. And we must not forget that the fact that in Shakespeare's day they had more need of it than in Marlowe's and in ours more than in Shakespeare's, is not altogether to be explained by a growing regard for truth and consistency in character. Abruptness in conduct also cuts the situation short, and spoils the harmony and rhythm of the whole. Above we have seen that Shakespeare himself was careful to smooth things over, even though he did not really motivate and prepare for Othello's fall.

[2] Pp. 114, 118.

[3] *Winter's Tale*, III, ii, 146-73.

[7] Examples abound, as in *Henry IV*, Pt. I, I, iii.

[5] *Richard III*, IV, iv.

[6] Gervinus and Fischer seem quite taken in by it, and the latter even declares that Richard does not dissemble! (Wetz, pp. 133-4). Even Wetz, who demurs, says, "Es setzt ein sehr grosses Seelenleiden voraus, wenn ein so harter Mann wie Richard zum Weinen und zu hoffnungsloser Verzweiflung gebracht werden konnte." (p. 125).

and psychological lore[1] in order to justify to us a method that the literary historian easily recognizes as customary and accceptable in Renaissance art, which had at command none of this lore, but intolerable in modern art, which has all of it.

Anne or Elizabeth is no more of the fifteenth century than of the twentieth; like the infinitely finer work in Othello, either is but a figure in sixteenth century dramatic art. Either inclines to marriage on persuasion, as Evadne, by another, still more expeditious and summary, convention, surrenders to virtue at the point of the sword.[2] *Tout se décide par la prière ou l'épée.* The game is always in the open, and is won or lost by persuasion or oratory, by force or threats of force. Even in those cases in which the struggle is internal, the Shakespearean character copes with himself in the same overt and face-to-face fashion. As in all Renaissance drama, the soliloquy given him is cast in the Senecan mould of apostrophe or question, debate or command.[3] And, however summarily, he disposes of his scruples, and comes consciously to a decision, before he acts. Never does he act irresponsibly like Arthur Donnithorne, who rode off to Gawain's to escape a meeting with Hetty, but, not to miss it, galloped "the devil's own pace back again;" or like Raskolnikoff, who had not taken his murderous project seriously, but when the clock struck seven started as if awaking from a dream. Of that undertow of passion and predilection which sweeps us—considering and debating, choosing or refusing—imperceptibly but irresistibly on to our purpose, Shakespeare, like all other drama or fiction before our day, could have known nothing at all.

And Claudio can find it in his heart publicly to shame and repudiate Hero as Molière's gallants do the coquette Célimène, merely for the situation —or the sensation—and the plot. There is damage done to his character in the process, just as there is to that of the gallants and Alceste by their disloyalty in bartering confidences, reading other people's letters, and lending a ready ear to calumny,[4] though in Claudio's case amends is made by his remorse. He cannot, moreover, have suspected Leonato of being privy to Hero's shame and of conspiring against his honor;[5] for Claudio himself never suggests such a thing, treats him with respect in the church, and, at the meeting afterward, Claudio's friend Don Pedro calls Leonato "good old

---

[1] Pp. 118-126. Such a notion, for instance, as that Anne has a primitive indifference to relatives and spouse, that revenge is incumbent upon her as a duty to herself and her family rather than to the murdered, and that therefore, like Ximena Gomez, she does well to marry and allay the feud. The text of the scene, of all the play, of every Elizabethan play in which revenge appears as a motive, shows how little of that notion Shakespeare entertained. Or, again, such a notion as that she admires his strength as women often admire it in those who maltreat them and in criminals.

[2] See above, p. 51, note 3.

[3] Cf. my article "Criminals" etc., and my article "Falstaff," p. 101.

[4] M. Lemaitre, I think, somewhere remarks upon this.

[5] As Wetz thinks, pp. 156-7.

man," and he himself is rude to him only in retort to his reproaches. And his derisive remarks about Leonato and his brother on a later occasion and his taunting of Benedick[1] are only a matter of the dramatists's playing the game of dramatic effect for all it is worth, until the peripety of exoneration and repentance is upon us. Before that Benedick must challenge him, and Benedick must be provoked. For the same reason, too, Leonato himself is made to turn against his daughter and threaten her life.[2] Shakespeare would have Hero stand on her wedding-day utterly alone and unbefriended, that Beatrice's love and loyalty may shine the brighter and have cause to call Benedick to their aid. Again and again it appears that theatrical effect, or the light and shade of the whole, is more precious in the dramatist's eyes than a character's integrity. But here he is not so careful as even with Capulet to make the utterance of parental rage compatible with the tenor of the part;[3] and it is taking a character for flesh and blood again to remark that in such trying moments we cannot expect a father to keep his feelings under control[4]—cannot expect a fine man to keep from at once believing the worst concerning his daughter and threatening her, life and limb! All that we can expect, to be sure, is that the playwright should keep the character under control, should not sacrifice it to the plot.

"He did not write for German professors," says Rümelin, "who turn the pages back and forth, and out of the scattered speeches of every separate character try to fashion a finished whole." "He regarded his plays as a lively and changing scene," said Goethe to Eckermann, "which should pass rapidly before eye and ear, and his only interest was to be effective and significant for the moment."[5] Proof of the truth of this opinion (if stated more moderately) we have found again and again as in former articles we have studied both Hamlet and Falstaff, particularly in the shifting of the great comic figure from the function of wit to that of dupe or butt.[6] Sudden conversions and lapses are only the most unplausible part of a system common in Elizabethan plays, least unplausibly carried out in *Othello,* most brilliantly and speciously in Beaumont and Fletcher, whereby the chief

---

[1] V, i.

[2] *Much Ado,* IV, i, 125-9; 192-3.

[3] Not that Shakespeare has motivated the change in Capulet from the point of view expressed in I, ii, 13-17 to that in III, iv, and after, but, once cause is given him to hasten the marriage, his jolly, boisterous nature is not incapable of his coarse rage on learning that his daughter declines the happiness which he has thrust upon her. Yet like Othello he changes in the making, and there is in him a gentle and sentimental strain at first (I, ii) that we do not find in the banquet scene and after, as the dramatist prepares us for his rage.

[4] P. 161. Even so, Wetz's charity goes far, for Leonato, otherwise a fine old gentleman, is prompt to believe her unchaste and threatens her with death twice over. See above.

[5] Eckermann's *Gespräche mit Goethe,* ed. Houben, p. 496. Cf. on the subject Creizenach (1909), IV, pp. 297, 299, 300. This was far truer of the English than of the contemporary French drama. Cf. at the last page cited the shrewd remark concerning the English made by Sorbière (1663): "Ils ne regardent qu'une partie après l'autre, sans se soucier du total."

[6] "Hamlet and Iago," "Falstaff," cited above.

characters, before all is said and done, run the whole gamut of emotions. In the last scene, for instance, from the death of Desdemona to the moment when Othello is himself again—

I am not valiant neither—

there are hardly two or three speeches together in the same key, but his mood changes from solemn pity to wild grief or desperate regret, to anger when provoked by Emilia, to incoherent mourning when again he remembers his loss, then to mournful self-justification, then to the wrath of revenge.

A like range of emotion is to be found elsewhere in the play. It is a great stroke of theatrical art, no doubt, whereby his solemn nobler self is summoned up before us at the beginning of the murder scene, to plunge once more into jealous rage; but the last we had seen of him, a few minutes before, he was raging at his worst.[1] Since, however, it was in the interval that the change took place, it does not trouble us, as does the question how in the scene where, at the beginning and the end, he plays visitor at a brothel, he could manage to soar up to the ideal heights from which he laments the "wreck of his faith and love.". A moment before he had what Desdemona calls a "horrible fancy" and "fury in his words," and now he gives voice to the anguish of his heart in the noble lines "Had it pleased Heaven" and the rest. Not that we ignore the difference between a play and a novel, or fail to remember that in the three hours' traffic of the stage there has always been, because of the need both of condensation and of stage effect, a far wider range of emotion than is probable in life. But in three centuries of approach to realism, or rather in three centuries of finer thinking and of search for a finer mode of expression to suit, that range has been narrowed, the boldness of modulation, or acuteness of contrast, has been subdued. And now dramatists preserve the mood and tone of a scene, just as they preserve, more scrupulously, the integrity of the character; and we must look to the "well-made" but tricky play of thirty or forty years ago for the same prestidigitation and kaleidoscopic change as here. Authors, like actors, then "made points," as the authors of the more popular stage do still, instead of presenting a character, from first to last.

Quite Elizabethan, we have seen, is the art by which the free-souled Othello and Posthumus pass under the cloud of jealous fury and at the end shine forth again. They are like many other abruptly and unreasonably jealous characters in Beaumont and Fletcher and Massinger; but no one of these playwrights ever presented the situation with such poetic effect, as if a calm, beautiful theme which had appeared at the beginning of a tempestuous symphony were made to steal upon us again at the close. For the supreme

---

[1] V, i, 30-36. So in *Philaster*, III, ii, and IV, iii, the hero enters rid for the moment of the jealousy with which when last we saw him he was beset, in order to give us the thrill of his plunging into it once again, deeper than ever.

poet it is not enough that Posthumus or Othello should put off their jealousy
like Philaster, as if it were a garment, but they must be clothed again in
their former dignity and tenderness, though now deepened and saddened.

> You gentle gods, give me but this I have,
> And cere up my embracements from a next
> With bonds of death . . .

cries Posthumus as he leaves his wife; and when in reconciliation he is received into her arms again, it is possibly not fanciful to think that
Shakespeare's art (in these later days to be sure not so certain) strikes
something of the same note, though chastened and subdued, as when, in the
lines admired by Tennyson, he has his hero murmur:

> Hang there like fruit, my soul,
> Till the tree die!

But in the case of Othello there can be no question, and the final speeches of
the hero recall the calm and grandeur of his speeches in the first act as
clearly as Lohengrin's farewell to Elsa recalls the high unearthly melodies
of his advent. Never was the dramatist a poet, an artist of artists, if not
here. In the first act not a line of Othello's but is, as they say, "in tone,"
in harmony with

> Keep up your bright swords or the dew will rust them,—

whether he is speaking to Iago alone, or to Cassio as he comes "with lights,
officers, and torches," or to Brabantio, or later, in immortal oratory, to the
Senate. Passion cannot shake him, or the dart of chance pierce him, and
a light word and a smile are on the lips of the god. Of character he has no
end—without much more psychology than there is in a painting of Titian's
or a dramatic melody of Mozart's. Character appears in the notions expressed only as in the lineaments drawn,—in image, diction, rhythm, as in
lines or colors or musical tones, without analysis or any concernment with
mental processes or subtleties in themselves. The mental processes are simple and on the surface; the thoughts themselves are no discovery and revela-
tion of truth; and all we can say is, that, under the master's touch, word and
figure, not unlike clay or color, take form and start up into life.

And in the second act and the third, though the splendor of the appari-
tion is now somewhat abated, he is the same, except for his hasty anger with
Cassio, until the hour of his ordeal is come. His foreboding on the quay
is such a foreboding as he might have had, if really he were to have one at
all, and his courtesy and dignity continue to be unfailing. But at Iago's first
questions, we have seen, his self-sufficiency collapses, at once he is excited,
and then adieu Othello! indeed. Not that the poet is now less than a poet,
or spoils the tone and harmony of the figure as he does its mental consistency
or psychology. If Othello, for such cause, could really rage, no doubt he

would do it in this big and imaginative vein.   Poetically he is still identical—
"the Pontic Sea," "the error of the moon which comes more nearer earth
than she was wont and makes men mad," "aspics' tongues," and the sibyl
in her prophetic fury, are not ill in keeping with "these nine moons wasted"
and "antres vast and deserts idle."   And again and again in the midst of
his sensual passion there are touches which recall his earlier self :

> Nor from my own weak merits will I draw
> The smallest fear or doubt of her revolt;
> For she had eyes and chose me.
>
>   No, not much moved,—
> I do not think but Desdemona's honest.
> But there where I have garnered up my heart,
> Where either I must live or bear no life . .
>
>   O thou weed,
> Who art so lovely fair and smell'st so sweet
> That the sense aches at thee, would thou had'st ne'er been born.

Others are, when Desdemona first appears after Iago has tampered with his
peace, and when Othello, light in hand, soliloquizes above her bed.
  The change, when the old Othello comes back with all his dignity
upon his head, though as yet without his calm, is at the moment when he
says:

> Nay, stare not, masters; it is true indeed . .

and after that he does not leave us.   But it is with line 243—

>   I am not valiant, neither,
> But every puny whipster gets my sword.
> But why should honour outlive honesty?
> Let it go all. . . .

that begins the solemn, poignant musical movement with which the tragedy
sweeps to a close.   Emilia speaks her dying words, and thereupon this theme
—the sword-motive Wagnerians might call it—appears again.

> I have another weapon in this chamber;
> It was a sword of Spain, the icebrook's temper—
> O, here it is. Uncle, I must come forth.

After an interval of challenging and parleying the motive appears once
more—

>   Behold I have a weapon;
> A better never did itself sustain
> Upon a soldier's thigh. I have seen the day, etc.

in great amplitude and volume; but his pride—as of a paladin—in his
weapon and in his glorious past lapses into a wail of misery, and the sword-
motive, which had seemed to signify defiance, turns, by a hint, to the motive
of suicide.

> Here is my butt
> And very sea-mark of my utmost sail.

But now there is a retardation and digression—his thoughts are diverted from the act to the horror, present and future, which impels him to it. Then come Iago's entrance, the wounding of him, and the wrenching of the sword away. Still the motive of suicide is uttered again, though darkly,

> I'd have thee live;
> For, in my sense, 'tis happiness to die.

But upon that ensues a longer digression. In tender words Othello and Cassio express their reconciliation, but Iago vows that from this time forth he never will speak word. "Well, thou dost best," says Othello, much the same spirit, amid his anguish, as he who, at the beginning, had replied to Iago's urgency, " 'Tis better as it is." The disclosure of several details of the villainous conspiracy follows, and Othello's grief at his own folly grows. Then, when Lodovico, reminding him that Cassio rules in Cyprus, requires the general to leave the room and close prisoner rest, the main trend of thought, the theme of suicide, is, though under cover, in the last unforgetable speech, resumed:

> Soft you; a word or two before you go.
> I have done the state some service and they know 't.
> No more of that, etc.

Again the motive of his pathetic pride in his glorious past, as it had appeared a few moments before, and, though without pathos, it had appeared in talking with Iago at the beginning, in the Senate Chamber, and on the quay at Cyprus; again the motive of his recent happiness, his present irremediable disaster. Suicide itself ends the speech, but in that there is for us no mere surprise or empty shock of horror. Over his brain memory holds sway, as with the dying: he looks backward, even as he looks forward to the memory that there will be of him. Though no one sees his dagger, his words breathe only of still desperation and farewell. But the point is that with delicate and various repetition and retardation of the theme, whether by the business of the sword, or hints of suicide, or reminiscences and anticipations in digression, the poet had made it apparent already that this was his "journey's end," his "utmost sail," and, as if it were in music, had prepared and reconciled our souls. And the chief point of all is that this whole final movement is an echo or reflux of that with which the play began. For here in his misery is Othello again as first we knew and loved him—in his pride, in his tenderness, even in his calm—though now by passion shaken and by the dart of chance pierced.

All this, and the play as a whole, is a feat of the imagination merely and of a cunning pen. What great play is more? "If the poet makes use of philosophic ideas," says Croce truly, "he does so only that he may change reason into imagination;"[1] and that he can achieve only when the ideas are no longer new, are not wholly his own. Hence of psychology, with its searching analysis, its devious and subliminal processes, its "stunning" and forcing of thought—its fleeing from thought itself—its undertow and unconscious self-deceptions, he could give us nothing, even if he had had it to give.[2] Even Browning, who, three hundred years later, had it to give, could not always manage to impart it to his readers—to say nothing of an audience—because, of truth embodied in a character, and so presented indirectly, an artist can give us only what was fairly ours before.

Why then with Shakespeare should this interest in psychology, the subtle analysis of character and the revealing of recondite mental processes— science and learning in short—be any longer the chief of our critical diet, as it was in the Renaissance with Homer? How primitive and unsophisticated it is not to consider Shakespeare only as a dramatist and poet, not to be content with poetry and drama (as we are with mere music in Mozart, mere painting in Rembrandt) and that, too, the poetry and drama, not of Browning or Ibsen, but of his own simple and spacious days?

> Maintenant il ne faut pas
> Quitter la nature d'un pas;

whereas Shakespeare often roamed many a league away from her, and was concerned, as Goethe says, only with the effect of the moment. But he is all that ever he promised to be—poet and dramatist from beginning to end. He may be concerned only with the effect of the moment in respect to the psychological consistency of his characters, but not always in respect to the poem or the play. We have traced the harmonious relation of the last scene to the first scenes, and in the last scene the fine gradation of effects, and repetition and interweaving of themes or motives, which almost reminds one of the *Master Builder;* and another fine gradation we might have traced in the five meetings of Othello with Desdemona after the temptation begins, the hero being in each more brutal and nearer murder than in the one before. We have traced in part, too, the poetic identity and unity of the characters, which is preserved to us despite default of analysis and reason. By the sheer potency of art Othello, Iago, Desdemona, and Emilia maintain, through all their incredible spiritual vicissitudes, their individual tone. And inconsistent, unpsychological though they be, their passions speak ever true. It is

---

[1] *Æsthetic*, English ed., p. 278.

[2] Of the mind flying off at a tangent or escaping from the impending thought I know no instance in Shakespeare, though others have found it in *Othello, Hamlet*, and *Julius Caesar* (see above, p. 37). Even Pinero in the *Second Mrs. Tanqueray* could make shift so to psychologize (as he lets Paula, in her blank despair, talk with Ardale about the flat they kept and the furniture in it) only by dint of a bit of exposition at the end. "What am I maundering about?" she cries as she pulls herself together. How then could Shakespeare, even if he happened to carry all modern psychology *in petto*, dispense with a comment like that? If he knew anything it was how to express himself, and make his point in the unelusive language of the stage.

this poetic identity, this fine differentiation of tone, this concrete and intense reality of utterance, to be sure, which people have mistaken for psychology itself. But how much more reasonable and profitable it is to dwell on the great emotional speeches, the great emotional situations, which though they hang not so closely and intimately together,[1] and to reality, as in a modern play, yet give us (which is the chief thing) unfailing "faith in the emotions expressed." "With truer accents than in Othello," says Bulthaupt, who has been beforehand with us in recognizing the lack of motivation in the character, "pain cannot groan or stammer, weep or wail."[2] And the first real critic of Shakespeare will be he who by his learning, his imaginative sympathy, and a gift of expression not inferior to Hazlitt's or Lamb's, shall teach us to feel this, as he leads us back out of the modern world into the poet's, in something of the divine simplicity with which the poet once felt it himself.

Time and again by readers of my skeptical articles I have been asked, as if I had been trying to pluck away the solace and mainstay of their souls, What, then, do you leave us? In intention at least, I might reply, all that the poet and dramatist left us, which is immeasurably much. Of a portion of that heritage of poetry and dramatic art we have just feebly spoken, but what of the characters as characters? On that head the merely destructive critic may perhaps be permitted a word more.

In the place of psychology and its subtleties the poet had an infinite tact, the artist's delicate, flexible, plastic touch. "The Shakespearean delineation of character owes all its magic," says Mr. Shaw, "to the turn of the line which lets you into the secret of its utterer's mood and temperament, not by its commonplace meaning, but by some subtle exaltation, or stultification, or shyness, or delicacy, or hesitancy, or what not in the sound of it. In short, it is the score and not the libretto that keeps the work alive and fresh."[3] It is mere art, as we have said, with which professors and critics, or the reading public for that matter, are not content; but, with all the psychology and enlightenment in their libretto, what, at last, have our modern dramatists, or, with none of it, the ancient, to keep their memory green, but art, but score?

Not that that is the whole of it, or that Shakespeare's art is mere style, mere rhetoric and music. He had the finest feeling for what belongs together—thought, image, sentiment, as well as phrase and rhythm to suit. We

---

[1] See my article "Anachronism" etc., and compare Mr. Galsworthy's remark in a recent article, "The New Spirit in the Drama," in the *Hibbert Journal* (1913). "Shakespeare's form was extraordinarily loose, wide, and plastic."

[2] *Op. cit.*, p. 223-4.

[3] *Dramatic Opinions and Essays* (N. Y., 1906), i, p. 24.

have seen this to be the case, at the first and at the last, with Othello, and it is
more or less the case with his other characters. This is not mainly, as has
often been declared, the fruit of realism and observation—though that too
as we shall see, he had not failed abundantly to gather;—it is in one sense
something deeper and in another something not so deep, the plastic, differentiating principle in art. It is the *poet's* gift, not that of a seer but of a
"maker." It appears in the fairies and Caliban, for which there was no
model, as clearly and happily as in the real men;—as in Falstaff and Iago,
for instance, and that does not make it the more likely, of course, that the
one was done from the life or that the other is fully within the limits of
nature.[1] How delicately the dimensions of Titania's passions are reduced
and drawn to scale—her resentment, her jealousy and affections—and the
quality of her pleasures then fitted to these:

> Full often hath she gossip'd by my side,
> And sat with me on Neptune's yellow sands,
> Marking the embarked traders on the flood,
> When we have laughed to see the sails conceive
> And grow big-bellied with the wanton wind.

And Caliban, a creature of the fancy (or, if that be too weak a word, of
the imagination) but the nearest approach to *Kulturgeschichte* that Shakespeare ever made, is, in the varied earthiness of his pleasures and conceptions,
and through all the range of his apparent contradictions—his lawlessness and
his instinct to worship and obey, his affectionateness and his vindictiveness,
his laziness, abusiveness, and murderousness, and his craving and ready
gratitude for human comfort and protection—he is as much a character, of
course, as Falstaff or Macbeth. His notions and his pleasures, his delight in
nature and his fear of it, his taste for berries, pignuts, and (more than all)
the "celestial liquors" of civilization, are as much in keeping as are the simple,
primitive words in which he gives them voice. When he thinks of offspring
he calls it "brave brood," and when he begs his new master to do his killing
for him, cries, "bite him to death," or "batter his skull, or paunch him with a
stake, or cut his weazand with thy knife." Everything belongs together,
in short, and the "monster" is no less than a character, not so much by dint
of psychological analysis, or even of any mere realistic observation, as by
virtue of that faculty which lends form to a statue, a picture, or even a song.
It was art, the plastic touch, observation but not uncommon insight or knowledge, that gave him being and shape.

In Caliban's case, as in that of the fairies and the great company of his
"human mortals," the poet nowhere shows his feeling for harmony more
finely or broadly than in the vein of humour which he bestows. As befits

---

[1] For the one see my article "Falstaff;" for the other, my articles "Criminals" and "Hamlet and
Iago."

beings so elemental Titania and Caliban alike laugh at what concerns sex, but Titania's laughter has all the delicacy of a sprite's and Caliban's all the grossness of a satyr's:

> Oho, oho! would't had been done!

Even more, perhaps, the poet shows the sweep of his vision, or rather the sweep of his own emotions, or the sweep of the hand that strikes the strings, by introducing, without a dissonance, a note of humor into tragic rôles. Unlike the heroes of the classic stage, his laugh and jest; and Hamlet's irony and sarcasm are as much a part of his character as are his melancholy and indignation, and the Fool's gibes and babblings find a fit place amid the ravings of Lear. But this combination presupposes no psychology or penetrating knowledge of life. It was, with the discord unresolved, one of the time-honored traditions of his stage, and if Shakespeare had not taken it up and resolved it, he would simply have left one of his songs unsung, one of the quests to which on every hand he was summoned, unachieved. What it presupposes is only that preëminence which Dryden long ago adjudged to him, "the largest and most comprehensive soul."

> Not deep the poet sees but wide,

averred the great critic who was still greater as a poet; and his words have particular truth when applied to our popular dramatic poet, "soul of the age" that he was.

Form was his chief gift, but knowledge of the world, not much otherwise than as Chaucer or the greatest of other dramatists knew it, came, of course, with this, hand in hand. He had the keenest of eyes for the types and individuals the world fashions. Enormous resources of observation stood at his beck and call to body forth, in either sex, in any of the three estates, all the seven ages of man, each of them invested with its particular "humour" or temperament. The dignity and pomp of kings and the simplicity and warped intelligence of clowns and boors, the bluffness of soldiers and the wiliness of villains, the buoyancy and innocence of youth and the quavering, maundering vehemence of age,—all this was the province which he took for his own, the inheritance to which he was born. Yet he was not called to present mere types like Jonson, or "paint the passions" in the eighteenth-century sense of the phrase, but to give an individual form and voice to each. Often he repeated himself; but neither Romeo nor Jaques is Hamlet, Falstaff is not Sir Toby, Valentine or Mercutio not Benedick. And this he has brought about, not, for the most part, by their ideas or opinions, still less by any newness or originality in these, least of all by anything individual in the processes of their thinking—save as the uncultivated flounder or go round in a ring—but above all by exhibiting, with exceeding deftness, their traits and temper in the trick of their speech. Even in classical style they may argue, wrangle or declaim, curse, lament, or apostrophize, but for all that, in the rhythm, the accent or intonation, the choice of word or figure, there is often something, of which the classics never knew, which stamps them.

Idiosyncrasies, as Mr. Shaw has somewhere said, were Shakespeare's forte, and indeed all the Elizabethans—playwright, satirist, and character-writer alike—eagerly amassed material to delineate the "humours." But no one of them could manipulate it like Shakespeare, for no one ever felt so keenly the characterizing force (as regards profession, rank, culture, mood or temperament) of phrase, figure, or rhetorical arrangement, or the rhythm of verse or prose. The repetitions of Falstaff as he rolls a jest under his tongue are not the repetitions of Quickly, or of my lord Chief-Justice, or of the Danish Prince. And the poet has a differentiating sense even for shades of the same feeling at different moments in one's career. We have already seen this to be the case in the changing phases of Othello. Mercutio, wounded, is game to the last gasp, the same wit who had made merry over Romeo's sentiment, the same fighting-cock who had irritated Tybalt; but though he dies jesting, without a touch of sentiment or solemnity, he scolds a bit, and the mirth ebbs out of his words like the blood out of his veins. And Lear groping his way out of the darkness of his madness to the light—Cordelia, with her heart melting within her, over him—where shall we find the like among the ancients, the Spanish, or the French? Voltaire's Lusignan, as he emerges from his score of years in chains, is, in an instant, an orator and every inch a king. Our great Englishman, like many of his Elizabethan compeers, has a poetic—an English—regard for times, seasons, and circumstances, and for the commonplace and humdrum which intrude into life however high. Not only does he not shrink from introducing into his tragic text the word handkerchief, which Ducis classically translated *bandeau,* and Capulet's remark to the ladies about corns on their toes, which Pope, strangely picking and choosing, amended to "corns on their feet" (to say nothing of that abundance of concrete phrase, homely, vulgar or affected, with which he constantly illustrated character or re-created time and place), but he does not shrink from reminding us on the stage that there are moments when the hero himself must come down to earth, to humor (as we have seen) and to prose. He has the old Roman tyrannicides talk like men in the street about the weather and the season as the fateful day is breaking, apparently neither making allusion to the "glorious dawn of liberty" nor taking flight from the "impending thought;"[1]

---

[1] To quote Coleridge on Hamlet. See above, pp. 37, 61. Taine is at this point far nearer the truth. "His heroes bow, ask people for news, speak of rain and fine weather, as often and as casually as ourselves on the very eve of falling into misery, or of plunging into fatal resolutions. Hamlet asks what's o'clock, finds the wind biting, talks of feasts and music heard without; and

and it would have been quite impossible for him to have a hero, after two days' absence, meet his betrothed with an oration of fifty lines from which all customary greetings or references to the separation were omitted.[1] In these breaches of "decorum" he observes, then, a higher decorum; even as the incursions and irruptions of comedy into tragedy are, in his best work, run together into a higher and ampler unity than is known to the classics, ancient or modern; or as the inconsistencies of Emilia's loyalty to her mistress and her readiness, "for the whole world," to forget her wedding vow, of Brutus's philosophic temperament and his impatience of interference from the jigging fool, and of many another character like them, do not, like the irreconcilable, theatrical contradictions in Othello, break over the confines of art, since they do not break over the confines of humanity.[2]

this quiet talk, so little in harmony with action, so full of slight, insignificant facts, which chance alone has raised up, lasts until the moment when his father's ghost, rising in the darkness, reveals the assassination which it is his duty to revenge." (*Hist. Eng. Lit.* Book II, ch. iv.) So far as the artist is concerned, to be sure, it is not chance alone that has raised these up, else they would find no place in art; but they are not to be credited to psychology. See above, p. 37, note. They are to be credited rather to Shakespeare's realization of character in all its homely and trivial details. Coriolanus, the oaken-garlanded hero, must, as Taine observes, "go wash" (I, ix, 67).

[1] See *Zaïre*, I, ii.

[2] What contradictions in Shakespeare are owing to the irregularity of life and what only to the irregularity of his own thinking and writing are questions too big to be answered here. But I cannot refrain from observing that it is neither scientific nor sensible to recognize the one source and not the other. That is what the Shakespearean does. If you cavil at a contradiction he falls back—as always—upon life, of which his poet's every line must be the transcript. He does not realize that the position is a dangerous one, and that at bottom it implies that these plays are not the product of art at all. They are, then, the record of an oracle, the vision of a seer. And that to my mind is his ultimate opinion—that this greatest of dramatists, seeing life steadily and whole, was free to cast off the trammels of artistic method and classical logic, and introduce what matter he pleased. "Out of character," as applied to his work, is consequently a term without meaning. You may complain of Polonius, as I have done ("Falstaff," p. 94), to the effect that, sensible enough at first, he is, in the second act and afterward, indeed an "ass;" and your Shakespearean friend will answer, as mine has done: "He puts a degree of asininity into Polonius because he has seen a degree of asininity in old statesmen, generally sensible enough." And the critic has no notion that this is beside the mark. But surely our dramatist has inadvertently shifted ground, and has turned a serious character into a butt, to serve his purposes with Hamlet. If he were but seeing life whole, he would not thus have robbed his statesman of wit and wisdom for once and for all. The inconsistent character, says Aristotle, "must be consistently inconsistent." Our playwright is writing a play, meeting the needs of his plot, keeping dramatic functions (serious and comic) distinct, even though on occasion he changes them; and shall his vaunted liberty from the trammels of classical logic consist in lifting a character out of one scheme—only to thrust him into another?

Something the same is to be said, if we could stop to say it, of the contradictions in Falstaff, Shylock, and Cloten (see Pellissier, pp. 210-11). "Der Hinweis darauf, dass es ähnliche Widersprüche in der Wirklichkeit gebe," says Creizenach very justly (*IV*, p. 324), "kann in solchen Fällen zur Rechtfertigung des Dichters nicht genügen." Yet it must be added that on the following page the great scholar shows leanings toward the mystical, romantic point of view of Grillparzer— "dass wir bei Shakespeare an die Möglichkeit nicht denken weil die Wirklichkeit vor uns steht." And he even quotes Schlegel: "Wissen wir doch in unsern Bekannten, wenn sie einige Tiefe und Umfang des Charakters haben, nicht immer mit deutlichen Gründen darzuthun, warum sie sich jedesmal unter besondern Umständen so oder so benehmen, ohne dass wir darum an dem Bestande ihrer Persönlichkeit irre würden." This now timeworn argument sounds a bit like that of the apologist for religion, who when you cannot accept his miracles and dogmas, reminds you that you cannot comprehend the law of gravitation or the flower in the crannied wall. But he

All this can be done without psychology—I mean the psychology of Ibsen as well as that of the schools—and with Shakespeare it is a matter of tact and touch and not at all of "your philosophy." Of the unconscious self-deceptions or fleeings from one's thought or purpose, commonly imagined, he knows nothing; of these there was then quite nothing known and there is nothing in his text. Hamlet spares the King at prayer for the reason given.[1] When Othello cries "Not a jot, not a jot!" in answer to Iago's remark "this hath a little dashed your spirits," he either deceives himself as the angry man does when he says he is not angry, or else is too proud to confess the truth. "I'faith, I fear it has," is Iago's rejoinder, and his opinion, together with the unmistakable evidence of Othello's speeches just before and after, makes it ours.[2] And as for subliminal processes, the nearest he or anyone else in Shakespeare comes to them is when Othello cries "Goats and monkeys!" on making his exit after striking his wife. It is an expression which possibly was meant to echo, almost mechanically, and sub-consciously, what Iago had said about the lovers being "as hot as goats, as prime as monkeys;" but since the lasciviousness of the two beasts was proverbial, the expression demands no such psychological interpretation, and, as used in his jealous rage, it was quite clear enough—and natural enough—taken by itself.

As the reader will have observed I have not been using the word psychology in the sense in which Mr. Archer has, for the purposes of criticism, distinguished it from character-drawing.[3] I have used it in the sense of mental consistency or inconsistency, and of those tricks and capers, those self-deceptions, masked movements, and extravagant errings of the human spirit, on which we have already touched. But if Racine is a psychologist, Shakespeare is one too. He too is not limited to human nature in "its commonly recognized, understood and accepted aspects," (if by that we mean nothing philosophical) but "brings hitherto unsurveyed tracts within the circle of our knowledge and comprehension." He too "penetrates to underlying soul-states" (if by that we mean nothing scientific or sub-conscious) ; and let us by all means have Richard II for a piece of psychology if Falstaff and the Nurse in *Romeo and Juliet* are, with no discredit to them, to remain pieces of character-drawing. But if psychology is also to mean what in the

and Schlegel and the scores of critics who have quoted and echoed him must themselves be reminded that your friends uncomprehended differ from either an incredible doctrine or an unplausible work of art in that very material respect that these latter, *ipso facto,* correspond to no reality, have no claims upon our attention whatever.

[1] Cf. my article "Hamlet and Iago."

[2] The self-deception, if such it be, is for the audience thus plainly marked and labeled as a point at which Othello's own testimony is to be discounted. It is not like the self-deceptions discovered by critics in the soliloquies of Hamlet and Iago, of which the dramatist gives no hint.

[3] *Playmaking,* p. 288-92.

passage from Mr. Archer, quoted above,[1] he appears also to make it mean, a distinction must be drawn. No one has more imaginative sympathy than Shakespeare; but he employs it by fits and starts, often neglects motivation and analysis, takes a leap as he passes from one "soul-state" to another, and, not content with the inconsistencies of life, falls into the contradictions of convention and artifice. As a whole, in the relation of Othello tempted to Othello untempted, the psychology of the hero is false, or might be said to be non-existent, just as it is non-existent in the whole convention of Iago's impenetrable hypocrisy and his bamboozling of all the cleverest people in the play. And yet, if illogical, irresponsible, fitful, but unflagging sympathy —the sympathy of the imagination—is the only test, Othello is as psychological a being as the hand of man has framed.

In any case, the characters are not the play. How long they have been be-essayed and lectured upon as if each stood in a dramatic monologue like one of Browning's, and a trait were to be found in every deed or syllable! And that is due to some lack of artistic sense in Anglo-Saxon and German criticism, which seeks in art meaning and reality more than form and beauty. The play—the whole—is really, if not mathematically, greater than the sum of its parts; it, above all, is what any great artist or dramatist tenders or considers; and if *Hamlet* or *Othello* is greater than any play of Molière or Sophocles it cannot in this respect be quite different. Neither are the characters, as is always being said or implied, the beginning and source of the plot. What they do, even what they say, is only in part their own doing or saying. "The *dramatis personae* do not undergo experiences in order to exhibit their characters," says Aristotle, "but it is because of what they are to go through that they are invested with characters."[2] If we are to trust the testimony of many dramatic authors his words are as true today[3]—a situation, not a character, is the author's point of departure—but they are true in a profounder sense of the Greek and Elizabethan dramatists, who fitted improbable old stories for the stage, than of ours who contrive stories of their own. Yet with them it is not merely the borrowed plot which causes in the character trouble and confusion, but again and again, as we have seen, the exigencies of dramatic effect, the requirements (as men then saw them) of the whole. Many a time the crude old story, as in Belleforest's or Cintio's tales, is, we have said, reasonable and free of contradiction, as in *Hamlet* or *Othello* it is not.[4] Indeed, all the problems in the character of Othello which we have been trying to solve have been those of the poet's

[1] P. 29, note 3.
[2] *Poetics*, vi, 10, Margoliouth's translation.
[3] I cannot undertake to give the evidence for this in the present study.
[4] Scholars need no evidence for the truth of this sta...ent. Rümelin, speaking of the "histories," goes so far as to say (p. 217): "Er weicht von seinen Quellen gewöhnlich nur darin ab, dass er sie in der Richtung des Phantastischen überbietet und ihre pragmatische Motivirung abschwächt." His improvements lay in compactness of structure, stage-fitness, vigor and beauty (rather than clarity or reasonableness) of conception.

own making, though still more of the critics' making, as instead of bridging the gulf of time they have jumped it. Even in a modern play, however, in which the action is, by critics at least, supposed to rise and flow out of the characters alone, they are not to be taken out of the web of circumstance, and the fabric of convention and structure, any more than the figures are to be cut out of a painting. Out of the pattern or the plot, they have no existence nor ever had any. "Details" as we treasure them in carbon prints, galleries of poetic portraits extracted and exhibited by lecturer or essayist—how at the sight of them Raphael and Shakespeare would have smiled or shuddered! Indeed, to their psychological or anatomical truth or integrity violence had often been done by the artist himself, in his preoccupation with his effects, with pattern and design. And if really we love art, if we love the truth alone, then the picture the poet has painted must, as much as in us lies, be mirrored in our criticism even as we fondly think was his vast vision of life upon his canvas—steadily and whole.

ADDENDA

P. 25, *add to note 2, at the end:* Really, Desdemona is like Erastus in the old play *Soliman and Perseda* (1592), who unreasonably reckons his Perseda's love to be "lost" when he loses the chain she had given him; and Othello, for all that he is "wrought," is like Perseda, who, seeking no explanation, flies into a jealous rage when she sees her chain about the neck of Lucina, though this lady (like Cassio in his relation to Othello) has not been her rival in love. It is wholly a matter of goods lost and found again, but that simple and everyday matter is past these sensible people's finding out!

P. 67, *add to note carried over from p. 66, at the end:* But like the combination of comic with tragic elements, this presentation of a character half-hewn, with all the accidentals of human life clinging to it, was a tradition of his stage (cf., above, p. 65); and Shakespeare, again, did not so much discover life as take up and perfect an artistic method. In the mysteries and in the Elizabethan dramatists generally, heroes and potentates take their ease, and almost anybody is free to step over the confines of his rôle and joke or gossip.